stress-free Sewing Solutions

BARBARA EMODI

A **NO-FAIL** Guide to Garments for the Modern Sewist

 C&T PUBLISHING

Text and photography copyright © 2021 by Barbara Emodi
Artwork copyright © 2021 by C&T Publishing, Inc.

PUBLISHER: Amy Barrett-Daffin
CREATIVE DIRECTOR: Gailen Runge
ACQUISITIONS EDITOR: Roxane Cerda
MANAGING EDITOR: Liz Aneloski
EDITOR: Karla Menaugh
TECHNICAL EDITOR: Debbie Rodgers
COVER/BOOK DESIGNER: April Mostek
PRODUCTION COORDINATOR: Zinnia Heinzmann
PRODUCTION EDITOR: Alice Mace Nakanishi
ILLUSTRATORS: Mary E. Flynn and Leo Booth
COVER PHOTOGRAPHY by Karen Veinot of Little Windows Photography
INSTRUCTIONAL PHOTOGRAPHY by Leo Booth
LIFESTYLE AND SUBJECTS PHOTOGRAPHY by Karen Veinot of
Little Windows Photography

Published by C&T Publishing, Inc., P.O. Box 1456, Lafayette, CA 94549

Library of Congress Cataloging-in-Publication Data

Names: Emodi, Barbara, 1953- author.

Title: Stress-free sewing solutions : a no-fail guide to garments for the modern sewist / Barbara Emodi.

Description: Lafayette, CA : C&T Publishing, [2021] | Includes index.

Identifiers: LCCN 2021004954 | ISBN 9781644030592 (trade paperback) | ISBN 9781644030608 (ebook)

Subjects: LCSH: Sewing.

Classification: LCC TT705 .E46 2021 | DDC 646--dc23

LC record available at https://lccn.loc.gov/2021004954

Printed in the USA

10 9 8 7 6 5 4 3 2 1

Dedication

For my granddaughter, Anika, who also needs to know how things are made

Acknowledgments

This book has been inspired by all those sewists who love to sew but didn't always love the results, or even the process. Finding ways for them, and for me, to sew with less stress and more enjoyment has been sort of a life mission. Few things make me happier than discovering, from my own experiments or the wisdom of other sewists, that there is an easier way to do things. This book is my collection of tricks for the tricky stuff.

You see, I just love sewing and I want you to, too. I started sewing when I was eight, made most of my clothes from when I was twelve. That's many hours and many garments, but look at what sewing has given me. I have never been bored, not one day of my life. I have never not been excited by the feel of fabric, never not delighted by a perfect button, never not entranced by the great beauty of machine stitches marching out from under my presser foot. Sewing has made me who I really am. It's time I said thanks, with gratitude for the craft and gratitude for all my compatriots in the sewing community. Community matters. It means so much to me that my family and friends modeled the garments. I am grateful to the very talented Karen Veinot for her ability to capture them, my neighborhood, and the sewing so well. Thanks, too, to Christina Pasquet of Patch Halifax for sharing her wonderful store and the site for the cover shot for this book.

Finally, I am particularly grateful for one special person. My amazing husband, Leo, who did the technical drawings and took the how-to photographs, made it all possible. When the pandemic gave me production challenges, he was the one who said, you know we can do this, and made sure we could. If you could have seen the photographic studio he improvised in our living room, made of dog fences wired together and of bristol board—well, you would understand how much that man does for us and what he means to me. He comes through for everyone always, particularly if it is a creative project. This book is as much his as mine.

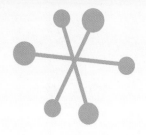

Contents

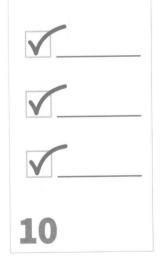

Introduction

This book is written for those who sew a variety of garment types for a range of people—themselves, friends, partners, children, and extended family. I am that kind of sewist myself. To do everything I want, I rely on my collection of tricks and maneuvers to keep my own sewing stress-free.

I want to share some of those methods with you. These are techniques that deliver first-class results but don't add performance pressure to the sewing experience. I want you to be delighted with your makes. I believe in ingenious sewing.

Defusing sewing challenges is mainly a process of finding new perspectives, not about fretting over your own skills. This is how this book works:

1. If something you've sewn doesn't turn out, flip through this book and find a *F.A.I.L.* (*Followed-All-Instructions Letdown*) that matches your issue.

2. Understand the why behind what went wrong.

3. Check to see if there is an immediate fix or rescue.

4. Learn strategies that will help you have the result you want next time. It's as simple as that.

My Principles for Stress-Free Sewing

- Think ahead to what can go wrong.

- Plan a detour around potential difficulties.

- Build in rest stops for fine-tuning.

- Remember there is always more than one way to do the same thing.

- Look at the menu of techniques and choose what works best for you.

Metric Conversion

The metric measurements in this book follow standard conversion practices for sewing and soft crafts. The metric equivalents are often rounded off for ease of use. If you need more exact measurements, there are a number of amazing online converters.

Chapter 1

Neckbands and Bindings

Humans search out faces. Necklines frame these faces. This raises the stakes for sewists. A messy neckline is the first thing anyone notices. Add to that, the Universal Laws of Sewing dictate: *If mistakes happen, they happen center front.*

Nicely covering that raw edge around a neckline matters, a lot. There are facings, of course, and these will be dealt with in another chapter. Many patterns suggest the edges in both woven and knit tops be finished with a binding or band. In theory, this should be easy. Pattern designers seem to think so. The reality is often more of a struggle. Hands up if you have ever had a bound edge that bowed out or a knit neckband that sagged in the middle. Me too. Fortunately, there are tricks that will solve your binding and neckband problems.

Bindings are narrow strips of fabric that wrap around a raw edge to stabilize, cover, and strengthen it. In garment sewing, bindings are used for scoop necklines or the armholes of sleeveless tops and dresses. In higher necklines, a bound edge is sometimes combined with back or front openings and closures—think a keyhole opening at the back of a top or a tie at the front of a blouse.

In knits, bindings are not the only way to finish necklines. Some folks suggest simply turning under the raw edge and stitching it down. This generally works in knits with a lot of body, such as scuba, and best if the edge is stabilized first with interfacing, fusible bias tape, or clear elastic. But my success rate with this technique tends to be about 4 out of 10. I like better odds in my sewing. So, I bind or use a knit neckband, a classic used in many knit tops of the T-shirt variety.

Let's get started.

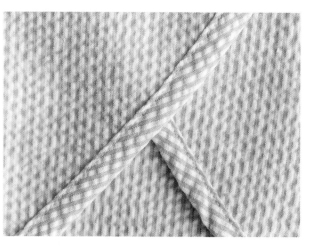

WOVEN BINDINGS

LOOK FAMILIAR?

The bound neckline in this woven top bows out.

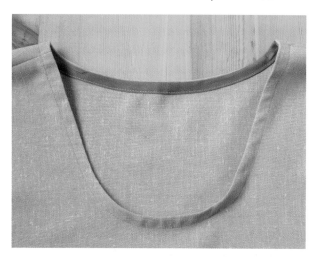

WHY THIS HAPPENS

This *F.A.I.L.* is just an example of geometry in action. The cut edge of the neckline is a curve that fans out into the body of the garment. As a result, a binding laid to match the smaller inner edge will pull in when turned and stitched down to the wider garment. Also, any binding made of fabric heavier than the fabric of the garment, as many purchased prefolded bias tapes are, can weigh down a neckline. That is part of the problem here.

NOTE: What Is *F.A.I.L.*?

F.A.I.L. = Followed-All-Instructions Letdown

Some instructions are harder than they need to be. It's not you; sometimes it's them. It's okay to seek out an easier way.

FIX IT RIGHT NOW

No amount of pressing is going to flatten this edge. The only real solution here is to take out the binding, press the cut edges flat, and apply a new turned and stitched binding as in one of the two Visible Binding Options (page 13).

A more radical solution, and one that is good for frayed nerves, is to unpick the topstitching and cut the binding off at the stitching line. Next, sew in a binding that shows, as in Visible Binding Options. The binding will fill in some of the lost space previously occupied by the cut-off seam allowance, and no one will be the wiser.

NEXT TIME

Whatever method you choose, following these four prep steps during construction will make all the difference.

Preparation Steps

STEP 1: STAYSTITCH THE EDGE

Staystitch the neck edge just within the stitching line, in two steps from each shoulder to the center front or center back. Without this staystitching, the bias of the curve will stretch when handling, adding to the gape issue.

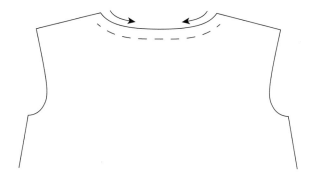

STEP 2: MAKE YOUR OWN BIAS BINDING

Make binding from self-fabric or, if the fabric is heavy like a linen, from a lighter-weight fabric. Cut 1¼″ (3cm) strips on the bias (*diagonal grain*) of fabric. Use a rotary cutter and a ruler and mat to cut, or use strips of masking tape on the fabric as a cutting guide. Piece the strips with diagonal seams.

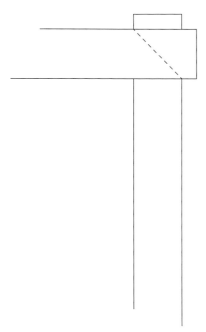

Tip DIY Versus Purchased Bias

The difference in quality is clear!

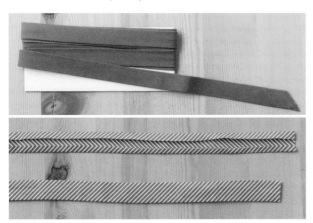

STEP 3: PRESS-SHAPE THE BINDING

Shape the binding with an iron to match the shape of the neck opening. Stretch the outer edge of the binding to form the curve as you press.

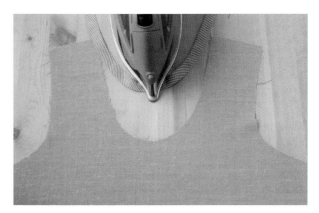

Tip Use a Bias Tape Maker to Shape the Binding

A bias tape maker can be a useful tool for shaping binding to fit an opening too. Just pull it in an arc as you press.

STEP 4: CLIP THE SEAM ALLOWANCE WELL BEFORE TURNING THE BINDING

See the difference between how flat a clipped edge lies compared to an edge that was not clipped, and as a consequence, pulls up? Make more frequent clips at the center front and along the curves.

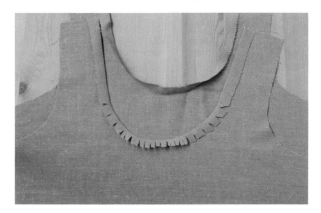

Choose a Binding Method

OPTION 1: HIDDEN BINDING

A hidden binding turned to the wrong side and stitched down. I use this on armholes and or on necklines of dressier garments when I want all binding evidence to be hidden.

Conventional method: Patterns often instruct you to stitch the binding into a ring that is stitched to the neckline, right sides together, then turned completely to the wrong side and topstitched. This was the method, as per instructions, used to make the _F.A.I.L._ It gapes, although staystitching, press-shaping, and clipping would have helped this neckline.

Unconventional method: Apply the binding flat to the opening first and then seam it along with the continuing construction of the garment. This is my favorite method. Here's why:

• Shaping the binding to the neckline is easier when the whole piece can be laid flat to work. Fine-tuning, like stretching the binding slightly at center front and center back to snug it, is easier this way.

• Stitching the binding around curves, using your fingers to spin the fabric under the needle as you sew, is easy with flat construction, harder with a closed garment. Flat sewing is less likely to distort grain and cause ripples.

1. Staystitch neck edges and armhole curves.

2. Stitch just one shoulder seam, leaving the other shoulder unstitched. _Note:_ If applying to an armhole, sew the shoulder seam and leave the side seams open.

3. Press-shape, pin, and stitch the binding to the edge of the neckline or armhole, right sides together. Stretch slightly at the curves. Clip into the seam allowance.

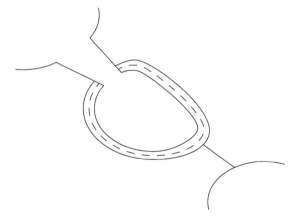

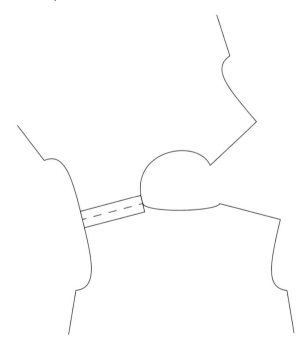

4. Press the seam allowances up into the binding. Stitch the remaining shoulder seam, or the side seam at the armhole opening, right up through the binding.

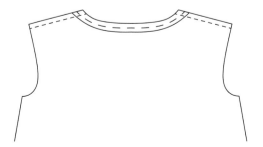

To do a first-class job with this last step, I usually machine baste the tiny juncture where the binding and garment seam intersect before the final stitching.

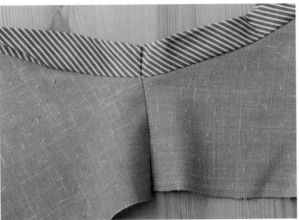

Right side of join

Back side of join

5. Turn the binding to the inside of the garment and topstitch down.

VISIBLE BINDING OPTIONS:
OPTION 2: VISIBLE BINDING TURNED TO THE INSIDE

This visible binding is hand stitched down on the inside. This is my go-to. Visible bindings significantly avoid the curve discrepancy issue, described above, and tend to hug the neckline better. The hand-stitching option eliminates any topstitching angst I might be having on the day.

1. Follow the Option 1: Hidden Binding, Unconventional Method, Steps 1–4 (previous page), for sewing a flat binding.

2. Trim and press the seam allowances up into the binding and wrap the binding over the seam allowance so the binding is visible. Hand stitch the binding in place on the wrong side.

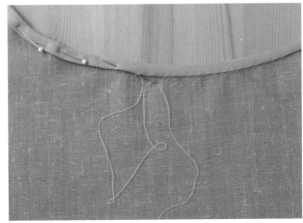

OPTION 3: VISIBLE BINDING TURNED TO THE RIGHT SIDE

This binding is topstitched down for a professional and durable finish. It's also fast, which is handy when there is a lot of binding to be done as in the pajamas (see pajamas photos, page 8).

Sew the binding in a ring first. This ensures that no raw seam allowances will be visible at the join.

1. Staystitch the neck edge, press-shape the binding, and pin the right side of the binding to the wrong side of garment neckline.

2. Stitch, trim, and then clip the seam allowances.

3. Press the seam allowances toward the binding and wrap the binding over the seam allowance to the right side.

4. Tuck under the remaining raw edge of the binding and topstitch in place.

Tip Accurate Topstitching

Use an edge-stitching foot to topstitch with fairly high accuracy and low stress. Butt the ridge of the foot right up to the binding and adjust the needle position so it is right on the edge of the fold. Too easy.

KNIT NECKBANDS

LOOK FAMILIAR?

This knit neckband has a definite gape at center front.

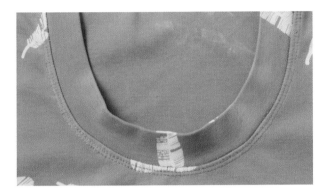

WHY THIS HAPPENS

This _F.A.I.L._ neckline was made using the pattern piece for the neckband. It was also made in one of the fabrics (cotton/LYCRA*) the pattern suggested for the top. Note how the band fits fairly well into the neck opening but seems too loose at the folded edge.

The issue here is that the top of the band next to the neck needs to be smaller than the edge where it attaches to the garment, so it can slope slightly into the neckline. This wide self-fabric band just can't retract enough to cup the neck.

Pressing the band would likely stretch the neckband even more. Making the neckband shorter, another possible solution, could cause the garment to pull in around the neck opening.

This top needs a completely different neckband.

* LYCRA is by INVISTA.

FIX IT RIGHT NOW

Apart from skipping right to the next section and starting from scratch, there are three options for quick, immediate fixes.

Option 1: Restitch the Same Neckband

To reduce neckband gap-osis, band width is as important as length. A narrower band has less discrepancy between the inner and outer edges of the band, so it will always lie smoother, particularly in self-fabric. One fix is therefore to simply restitch the band. No need to remove it; just take in a wider seam allowance. Accordingly, I reduced the band width in the top below from the pattern's 1¼″ (3cm) band to ½″ (1cm) by reserging around the original neckline. Even though this top was made with the same pattern as the _F.A.I.L._ example, see how much more smoothly this neckline lies.

Option 2: Add a Small V to the Neckband

Sew a faux miter by stitching a small dart through the band to make the V at the center front. The process is simple.

1. Fold the garment in half along the center front. Pin that fold in the neckband above the stitching line.

2. Using a small stitch length and not backstitching at either end, sew a small dart up through the band, keeping the line of stitching even with the center front fold of the garment. Leave tails of thread at each end of the stitching for tying off later.

3. Working from the right side, distribute the body of the dart evenly behind the stitching line. Thread the tails of thread through a hand-sewing needle and secure the end of the stitching, adjusting or closing the seam a bit if required.

4. Lightly press with a pressing cloth from the right side to finish.

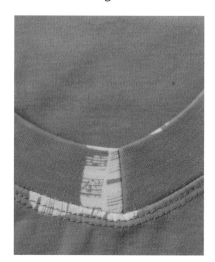

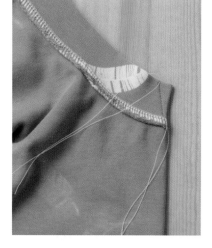

Option 3: Decide You Really Want a Cowl Neckline

A cowl is an excellent solution when it is already past bedtime and you are beside yourself with a baggy neckband. To add a cowl, just cut the whole upsetting band off, seam allowances and all, and find a decent-size scrap of leftover fabric.

1. Draft a pattern for your cowl neckline.

• **Width:** Measure around the newly liberated neckline and add two seam allowances. Cut with the degree of greatest stretch going across the cowl pattern piece. Cowls are sewn 1:1 with necklines, so there is no need to make them smaller as you would with a neckband. If you intend to lay the pattern on the fold of fabric, divide this total measurement by two.

• **Height:** Measure from the neckline to just under your chin. Double this measurement to accommodate the fold at the top of the cowl.

- **Angle:** Adjust the angle of the cowl so it will be closer to the neck at the top where it is folded. Measure about 1″ (2.5cm) in at the fold line, halfway up the height of the cowl. Draw out from this point, above and below, to make a wedge-shaped indentation in the cowl seam. This little dip will help the cowl hug the neck a bit.

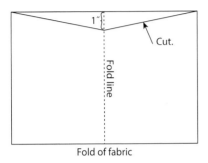

Fold of fabric

2. Sew the cowl into a ring. Fold the ring in half, wrong sides together, and stitch the cowl to the neck opening. Since this is a knit, you can leave the seam allowances as is, or zigzag or serge to finish them.

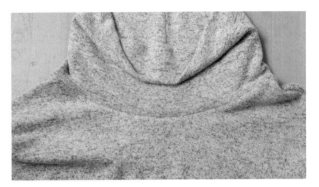

NEXT TIME

Figure Out Your Own Band Dimensions

Everything depends on the fabric, and the stretchability of knit fabrics is hugely variable. Guidelines are helpful but that's all they are, starting points. Instead I am going to give you some ratios to work with. Even when you use the ratios, I suggest you first baste in the neckband, assess the results, and fine-tune as necessary. Sometimes I experiment with two or three configurations before I feel I have the perfect band-to-neckline ratio.

- **Band width:** Make any neckband cut from the same fabric as the garment fairly narrow. A neckband from self-fabric cut to a finished width of ½″–¾″ (1–2cm) will lie smoothly.

- **Band length:** There is no standard formula. There is a big debate on social media—the 85% folks pitted against the 75% folks—but knits don't live in an environment of absolutes. Stretchy knits require less length; less stretchy knits require more. Let your own hands and eyes tell you what works best.

When the garment and the band are in the same fabric, start by cutting the band length three-quarters the dimension of the opening, and adding two seam allowances. Then baste and test the band.

Tip **Use the Quarter Method**

To evenly position the band into the neck opening, place marking pins at the quarter points of the neckband and of the opening, then use clips to secure.

Use Ribbing for the Band

Ribbing is stretchier than most garment fabrics and does a naturally better job of cupping the neckline. A ribbing band can be much wider, by ½″–¾″ (1–2cm), than a self-fabric band and still lie nicely. And because ribbing is so stretchy, the ratio of band to opening is less. A measurement of two-thirds of the neck opening for the band length works very well for ribbings.

The neckband of the top below is the same width as the band in the _F.A.I.L._ sample, but notice how much more smoothly it lies, because the neckband here is made of ribbing.

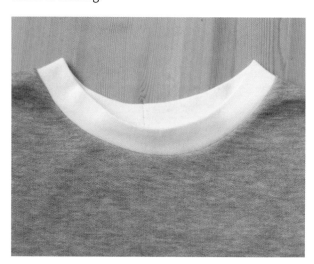

Install the Band Flat

In purchased tops, the neckbands or sleeve bands are often applied in the flat. The last seam is run up through both the garment and the band. The seam allowance later is tacked to one side.

The cozy home sewist can do the same for these reasons:

• It's fast. This is obviously why this is a preferred factory method.

• It gives great control when testing ratios of neckband-to-edge stretch. Often, I use a longer-than-necessary band piece, pin it on so it pulls the neckline in nicely, and cut off the excess. Very efficient.

1. Leave one seam unsewn—the sleeve seam for a wrist band or a shoulder seam for a neck band. Fold the band wrong sides together and stitch it along the right side of the flat edge—along the bottom of a sleeve or along the neck edge.

2. To close up the band, stitch the last seam of the garment, right through to the band.

3. To neaten the join, stitch the seam allowance down to one side, by hand or by machine.

KNIT BINDINGS

This knit binding has distorted the neckline. Attempts to press it out made it worse.

This terrifying _F.A.I.L._ is the result of two things: The first is a many-layer construction technique that made the binding outweigh the garment fabric. The second is a method of application that over-handled both fabrics, stretching them out, and then permanently stitched in that shape.

Cut it off and throw it out the window. I have done just that. Feels great. Then rebind using one of the two approaches under Next Time.

Or you can replace the binding with a narrow neckband (see Figure Out Your Own Band Dimensions, page 17) that will look like a binding. Just make sure the neckband is wider than the seam allowance behind it.

Method 1: Double Binding

In this method, a folded binding—not unlike a band—is stitched right side to the wrong side of the garment and then topstitched down. Since turning under a raw edge on a knit and topstitching it from the front can be tricky with a stretchy fabric, I most often use this method. Since the band is doubled, it is best for light fabrics or bindings lighter than the garment fabric, such as meshes.

1. Sew the binding into a ring and fold it in half, wrong sides and raw edges together.

2. Pin the right side of the folded band to the wrong side of the garment.

3. Stitch and trim the seam allowance to reduce bulk.

4. Turn the binding to the right side of the garment and topstitch close to the outer folded edge of binding. To topstitch evenly, use an edge-stitching foot. See Tip: Accurate Topstitching (page 14).

Method 2: Single-Layer Wrap Binding

This can be used in any weight of fabric and is the only viable binding option for medium to heavy fabrics. Once wrapped, the binding can be stitched down from the right side in-the-ditch, as was done here. This method can be used with a ring of binding, but I find it 900% easier if it is done in the flat. Your call.

Knits don't fray, so you don't need to turn under the raw edges. When wrapping and binding an edge with knit fabric, I always cut the binding wider than I need. It is so stress-reducing to have something substantial to hold on to while I sew. I just trim off the excess when I am done.

1. For a neck binding, stitch one shoulder seam. For armhole bindings, stitch both shoulders but not side seams. This is very similar to the Option 1: Hidden Binding, Unconventional Method (page 12), for woven bindings.

2. Right sides together, pin and stitch a single layer of binding to the garment edge.

3. Stitch the remaining garment seams—the shoulder seam or the side seams—toward the binding so the seam allowances are folded into the binding. The seam will look like this from the inside:

And like this from the outside:

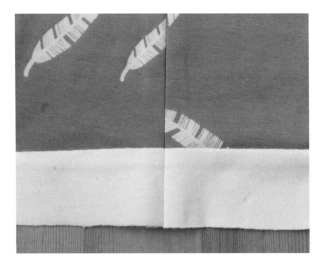

4. Stitch down the binding from the right side, using one of the following methods.

• **Ditch stitching:** Typically, sewists were advised to spread the fabric on either side of the binding seam with their fingers and situate the topstitching right in the well of the seam (in-the-ditch), where it will be invisible. This is tricky. Instead, I use a zipper foot to get the stitches close to and even with the binding. After stitching, I trim away the excess binding from the wrong side.

- **Topstitching:** Use a twin needle (see Twin-Needle Hems, page 152) and straddle the seamline.

- **Topstitching with a coverhem or cover stitch machine:** To reduce seam bulk, when the seam will be covered with a cover stitch, I sew the binding on first with a narrow zigzag on the sewing machine before cover hemming.

Method 3: Industrial Flat Binding

This is the standard method for bindings attached with either a domestic or commercial coverhem, also known as a cover stitch machine, so the edges are completely bound with coverhemming before the structural seams are sewn. Many brands of domestic coverhem machines have a binding attachment that applies, turns, and coverhems the binding in one operation. If you don't have this attachment (my brand doesn't make one), you can use your coverhem machine to do the topstitching steps in either of the two methods described above.

Tip Use Wooly Nylon

In all three cases, use wooly nylon hand wound in the bobbin to keep the stitches flexible and flat.

Chapter 2
Facings

Facings are often the smallest pattern pieces we cut, yet they can be the biggest of sewing nuisances. The idea is simple enough. The facing's only job is to finish the raw edge of an opening and provide a little support. However, we have all had facings that flipped up, facings that added a hard ridge to a neckline, and facings that—after fourteen tries to tack them down—still puckered and pulled along the seam allowances.

The truth is, those familiar kidney-shaped facings are often optional. Garment manufacturers often make their facings larger, eliminate them, or replace them with linings or bound edges (see Chapter 1: Neckbands and Binding, page 8). Folks who sew for themselves can often do the same.

The first question to ask: Is the facing really necessary? The answer in some garments is "absolutely." A shaped neckline usually has to be faced, and some edges like the front facings in tops, jackets, and coats need them too. However, back neck facings in blouses often are unnecessary and can be replaced by bound seams, yokes, and even serging/overlocking.

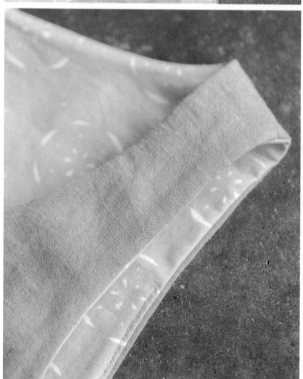

Multiple facings, for necklines and armholes in sleeveless tops and dresses, are another elective detail. I like to merge mine into single units that are less bulky and faster to apply. I also find they give my garments a sleeker finish and are just more fun to sew. Improving, or redrafting and replacing, standard facings is easy.

SEWING TIPS FOR FACINGS THAT DON'T SHOW

Some sewing issues seem to show up only when you have been wearing the garment for a while. A facing that is perfectly flat on the sewing table can flip, pull, or even stick out when you are out and about. How many of us have had a well-meaning family member or even a stranger reach over and tuck in a facing for us?

LOOK FAMILIAR?

This *F.A.I.L.* top looks lumpy where the armhole and neck facings meet at the shoulder seam. The neckline pulls forward at center front and the facing shows along the seamline.

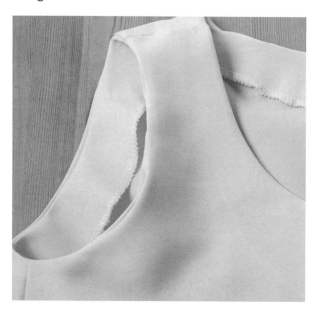

WHY THIS HAPPENS

The seams of the facing, stacked over the structural seams of the garment, keep this neckline from lying flat. Also, a facing that curls forward a bit like this indicates a seam allowance that needs to be clipped well along the curves, and interfacing should be removed from the seam allowances.

FIX IT RIGHT NOW

You won't be able to press this particular facing into submission. These facings need to be removed and redrafted to eliminate the shoulder seams. In the armhole facing, the underarm seams should be offset from the side seams of the garment.

Tip Consider Thinner Fabrics

Facings do not have to be made with the garment fabric. In some thick fabrics, such as a bouclé, self-fabric facings would be too bulky and show through on the right side of the garment. Instead, opt for a good match with thinner fabric—a dupioni facing under a silk tweed, for example.

NEXT TIME

Facings don't need to have seams exactly where the garment does. A facing's job is not to mirror, but to cover. Redrafting a two-piece facing into one, and offsetting necessary seams will make a huge difference.

Turn Two Facing Pieces into One

NECKLINE FACINGS

1. Lay the front neckline and the back neckline (or the front armhole and back armhole) pieces together with the shoulder seam stitching lines on top of each other. Pin or tape together.

2. Note the grainlines for the front and back pattern pieces may be different. Follow the grain for the front piece to cut out a new, single piece.

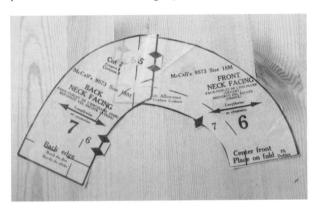

ARMHOLE FACINGS

1. Match the shoulder-seam facing pieces with the stitching lines on top of each other. Pin or tape together.

2. If you are working with heavier fabrics, move the underarm facing seam to the back by 1″ (2.5cm) to avoid stacked, bulky seam allowances under the arm.

  A. At the underarm of the back facing piece, mark a new stitching line 1″ (2.5cm) in from the original stitching line. Mark a new cutting line 1″ (2.5cm) in from the original cutting line.

B. Tape the front facing piece to the back facing piece at the underarm seam, matching the original cutting edges.

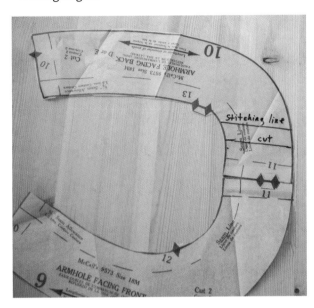

C. Cut the two facings apart at the new cutting line.

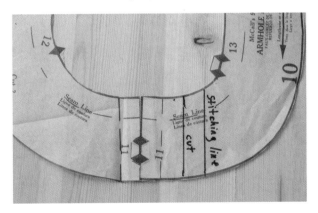

3. Cut a new one-piece facing, referring to the grainline of the front facing to lay out the new piece.

Offset the Facing

In thicker fabrics, cutting the facing slightly smaller than the garment will help it roll to the inside and stay. There is no need in thin fabrics, which should fold over the seam quite easily.

No fancy trimming of the facing piece is required; you can do this at the machine with the regular facing piece. Start pinning the facing to the edge, but with the facing underneath the garment. As you pin, extend the facing slightly, just a smidge, past the cut edge of the garment. When you stitch the seam, make sure you use the cut edge of the garment, not the raw edge of the facing, as the seam guide. Remove this little extra facing fabric in subsequent trimming and grading.

To help facings roll to the wrong side at shoulder seam areas in thicker fabrics, increase the facing offset a bit more just in that area. Consider fabric thickness, and turn of cloth, when you decide how far to extend the facing away from the opening.

Tip **How to Stitch Smooth Curves**
Shorten the stitch length from a 2.5 to a 2.0 or even 1.5 for smoother curves.

Understitch

To reduce bulk in the seam allowances and help the facings to stay hidden, prepare the seams for pressing in the following order. For a facing that truly stays put, make sure there isn't any interfacing in the seam allowance.

1. Grade the seam allowances (see Grade, page 163). Trim them both and then trim the seam allowance closest to the facing a little bit more. Stepping the seam allowances will keep them from showing on the right side as a ridge.

2. Clip into the seam allowances, clipping more frequently at the most curved edges, like the center front of a neckline. This is the secret to facings that lie flat.

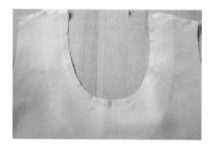

3. Working from the right side, hold the facing and seam allowances together and understitch (page 164) near the seamline. This helps the facings roll to the wrong side.

4. Attach the facing to just the seamline of the garment with a few flexible catch stitches (page 165). Resist the temptation to pull these threads tight, as this can create puckers on the right side of the garment.

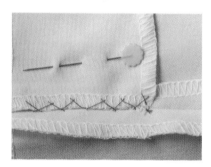

Neck and Armhole Combo Facing

It is a fact of good dressmaking that the less bulk on the inside, the better the garment looks on the outside. Really smooth sewing depends so much on trimming, grading, and notching, and on eliminating unnecessary seams whenever possible.

Nix those nonessential seams in your facing construction. Redrafted, streamlined facings give you a nicer result, and they save sewing time. We did a little of this when we merged the shoulder seams of the front and back neck facing pieces (see Turn Two Facing Pieces into One, page 25), but the neck and armhole facings can be entirely combined too. This is a great technique for sleeveless dresses.

DRAFT ALL-IN-ONE FACINGS

I would use this method to face a classic sheath dress with a back zipper opening or a pullover top or dress with some shoulder width. Because there is no need to tack down the facings at the shoulder seams, these integrated facings give a nice, smooth finish to the neckline and shoulder.

In a top or dress without a center back seam, I recommend two facing pieces, combining neck and armhole facings, one for the front and one for the back. In a top or dress with a center back seam, often with a zipper closure there, you will need three facing pieces—one for the front and two for the back. Just make sure you allow for a seam allowance at the center back.

These unified facings truly fade into the background in a dress, which is exactly what a good facing should do.

To draft a single front and single back facing pattern:

1. Lay tracing paper over each of the front and back garment pattern pieces.

2. Trace around the necklines, armholes, and down a bit along the center front fold line and the center back.

3. Mark a point about 2″–3″ (5–8cm) below each armhole stitching line. Mark a similar distance down from the center back and center front neckline stitching lines. Connect the underarm and center front marks.

In the pattern below, it is clear how much the original separate facing pieces would have overlapped. The single facing has eliminated all that unnecessary bulk.

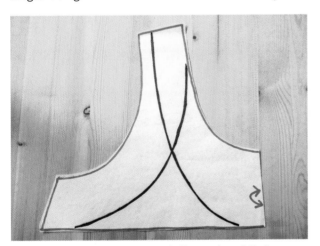

The tracing paper was folded in half to make a full-size pattern. The black lines show where the original armhole and neckline facing pieces would have been. The red lines outline the new single front facing piece.

Tip Extra Ease at Bust

If you have a large cup size, or just want some extra ease, draw the line at the bottom of this single facing piece with a bit of an arc up at center front to give room for the bust and shoulder blades.

4. Cut out and finish the lower edges of the two facing pieces.

FACINGS IN SLEEVELESS GARMENTS
Garments Without a Center Back Seam

For this method to work, sew the shoulder seams but not the side seams before you apply the facings. It is also important that the shoulders are not too narrow—at least three-fingers wide. You will need this room in the shoulders because eventually the entire garment will need to be pulled through this space. For narrower shoulders, see Garments with Narrow Shoulders (page 30).

1. Stitch the garment shoulder seams. Press.

2. Stitch the facing shoulder seams. Press.

3. Right sides together, pin the facing unit to the garment around the neckline, remembering to extend the facing just a smidge beyond the cut garment cut edges. (This will help the facings roll to the wrong side.) Stitch.

4. Trim, grade (page 163), and clip the seam allowances. Understitch (page 164).

5. Turn the facings to the inside and press.

6. *This is an important step.* Smooth the facing and pin to the armhole edges just to check that they meet accurately. It is not unusual for the one layer, the garment or the facing, to be a little smaller or larger after all this stitching, turning, and pressing. Since the these cut edges will need to match exactly, do any trimming now to make sure they are the same size.

7. Flip the garment over to the wrong side, so the right side of the finished facing will be facing you. Before you stitch the armhole edges together, you need to roll the garment up tightly so the facing and armhole edges can be wrapped around and pinned. Start by rolling one side of the garment up almost to the opposite side of the neckline.

8. Wrap the facing and armhole edges around the rolled-up garment, right sides together. Pin and stitch. Trim the seam.

9. Reach into the facing and pull the rolled fabric through and out. Repeat this process on the other facing edge. Press. Presto. A beautiful facing.

See how neat the shoulders look with these all-in-one facings? A complementary fabric adds a nice detail too.

10. Right sides together, sew the side seams of the garment and the facing together in one long, continuous seam. Because it is really important that the underarm seams of the facing and garment line up, I usually baste this section of the seam and check it before I do the final stitching.

Garments with a Center Back Seam

1. Sew the shoulder seams of the garment (plain fabric below) and facing (striped fabric below) units. Pin the facing to the garment, right sides together. Stitch around the neckline and armholes. Grade (page 163), clip, and understitch (page 164), these seams as far as possible.

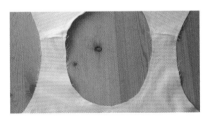

2. Reaching through from the front, pull each of the back pieces through the shoulder seams to the right side.

3. Press the garment, taking care to roll the facings to the wrong side.

This is the facing completed from the right side. Such a nice clean finish.

4. Right sides together, sew the side seams of the garment and facing together in one long continuous seam, basting the intersection of the facing and garment seams at the underarm before committing to the final stitching. See Garments Without a Center Back Seam, Step 10 (above). Turn and press.

Tip **Easy Transition to a Full Lining in Sleeveless Dress**

This method for facing a sleeveless garment can be used to insert a full lining into a sleeveless dress. Just think of the lining pieces as long facings, and you are set.

The back seam in the lining can be stitched after the lining (facing) is in, and the sides of the opening above this seam can be hand stitched to the zipper tape.

Note, however, that interfacing in a lined, rather than faced, dress is applied directly to the wrong side of the garment. Baste a woven interfacing to the neck and armhole edges and pink the other edges of the interfaced pieces to avoid show-through.

Garments with Narrow Shoulders

In a garment with very narrow shoulders and a one-piece back, such as pullover tops and dresses, the pull-through method for a one-piece facing won't work. There simply isn't enough room for all that fabric to be pulled through a narrow shoulder channel.

In some pattern instructions, the faced and completed front and back shoulders for garments like this are stitched together in a sort of a circle working from the inside. In theory, this approach is a great idea. However, it can be very tricky to hold the cut edges together during the stitching, unless you have tiny hands like Barbie. I don't.

I think it's a lot easier to just slide one shoulder up into the other and simply stitch them together across with one short seam. This method begins from a fancier version of the all-in-one facing. It is slightly more involved, but just as magical.

To face a narrow shoulder garment, start by drafting, cutting, and preparing the new facings. Because these narrow shoulder garments tend to be light, interfacing is optional. Use your judgment.

Note that, in this method, unlike other versions of the all-in-one facing, the shoulder seams are not stitched before the facings are applied.

1. Make an all-in-one facing pattern piece (see Turn Two Facing Pieces into One, page 25) for both the front and the back. If you wish, you can extend the facing to just above the bust or make it even longer to become a free-floating underlayer or lining.

2. Cut one front and one back facing. Finish the edge of the facing pieces. For this light silk, I just rolled the hem on my serger. For other ideas on how to hem fine fabrics, see Chapter 9: Hems (page 144).

3. Right sides together, stitch the facing to each front and back piece, around the neckline and around the armholes. Double-check that each shoulder strap area, between the stitching lines, is exactly the same size. These will have to fit together smoothly later when the shoulders are stitched together, and any discrepancies will really show.

4. Trim, grade (page 163), and clip all seam allowances. Understitch (page 164) the facings to the seam allowances as far as possible.

5. Turn one of these units to the right side and press (it doesn't matter if this is the back or the front).

6. Slide the right-side-out unit inside the wrong-side-out unit, with the outer layers next to each other. Make sure you don't have one outer layer and one facing layer next to each other. You will find those long serger tweezers handy here. Double-check that you have the outer layers together and facing layers together before the next step. One of my learned-the-hard-way lessons.

7. Stitch the two units together at the shoulder seams, through all layers. To make this easier to see how one fits inside the other I have extended the inner unit in this picture.

8. Turn the whole garment to the right side. Right sides together, sew the side seams of the garment and facing together in one long continuous seam, up from the hem of the garment to the bottom of the facings, pivoting slightly as required at the underarm. Since I was working with light fabric, I sewed this seam with a serged/overlocked rolled hem to reduce seam-allowance show-through on the right side.

Press.

ELIMINATING BACK NECK FACINGS

Back neck facings in blouses have long been on my hit list. We all know they don't tend to stay put. Even more annoying, in most cases, they are not structurally necessary. Fortunately, you don't really need them at all.

LOOK FAMILIAR?

This facing wanted to flip up. The tacking stitches attaching the shoulder seams pucker and pull.

WHY THIS HAPPENS

A facing like this one—finished, interfaced, stitched, and attached—is overkill. The only job of this facing is to cover the raw edges for a few inches at the back of the neck. And it's breaking one of the first rules for smooth sewing, that the underlying pieces should never be heavier than the main garment.

FIX IT RIGHT NOW

To rescue this *F.A.I.L.*, unpick and remove the facing. Finish the raw edge at the back of the neck with a simple line of serging or binding.

NEXT TIME

Tape/Bind the Back Neck

In ready-to-wear clothing, often the back neck facings are replaced with an applied taped edge or a self-fabric binding. It is so easy to do this yourself.

1. Sew the shoulder seams of the blouse and stay-stitch and clip the neckline (page 162).

2. Throw the back neck facing piece in the waste basket.

3. Sew, grade (page 163), turn, and press the collar. Topstitch as required.

4. Sew the front facings to the front edge of the garment only, not the neckline.

5. Cut a length of bias binding about 1½″ (4cm) wide and about 2″ (5cm) longer than the distance along the back neck from facing to facing. Press one long edge under ¼″ (6cm).

6. Pin the collar to the neck edge of the blouse. Wrap the top edges of the front facings around the collar, turning under the seam allowance where the facings would have been sewn to the back neck facing. Pin and stitch. Trim the seam allowance.

7. Lay the bias binding right side to the wrong side of the garment, with the cut edges of the neck edge and the binding even. Extend the binding in a bit to hide it under the edge of each facing. Pin and stitch the binding in place over the previous stitching line, being careful not to catch the body of the garment. I find it easiest to sew with the garment turned over so I can follow the previous stitching line. Trim away the excess seam allowance.

8. Turn the binding down and topstitch the binding to the back neck edge, starting and ending a little past each shoulder seam. Press. Turn the facings to the right side and continue with construction.

Tip Finishing with Tape or Serging

You also could finish the back neck by topstitching on a finished tape, this is common in golf shirts, or by simply serging, not binding, the back neck seam.

Serging a back neck is one of my favorite relaxed sewing techniques.

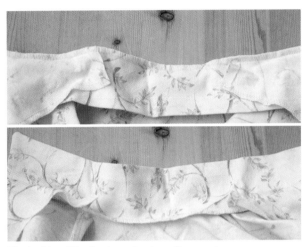

The inside of the back neck edge after serging

And from the right side of the garment. See how smooth and minimalist this treatment is, versus the bulk of a traditional back neck facing.

YOKE IT

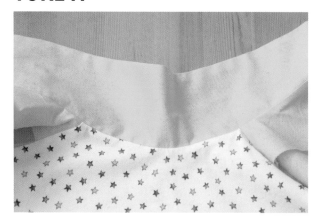

In many ready-to-wear blouses and jackets, back neck facings are morphed into much neater yokes, while still maintaining conventional front facings.

This is an easy adaptation to make. I really like to do this when making unlined casual jackets, where the flipping-up tendency of back neck facings can be particularly annoying.

1. Measure from the back armhole and place a mark one-third to halfway down the garment from the shoulder seam. Draw a line from this mark across to the center back. This is the yoke pattern piece. Trace it and add a seam allowance to the lower edge. Cut two yoke pieces from fabric.

2. Trace a lower back pattern piece from this line down and add a seam allowance to the top edge. (If you would like some extra shoulder ease, you can add a small pleats or areas of gathering under each shoulder blade.) Cut one lower back piece.

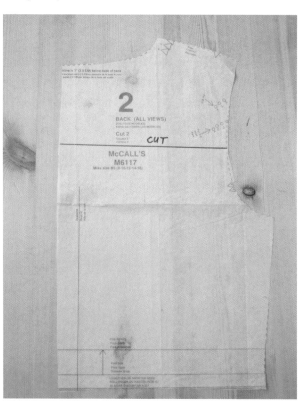

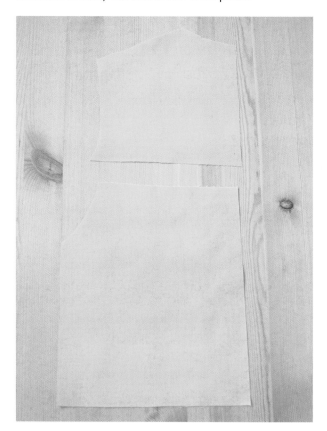

The construction method for completing a yoke/back facing for a blouse with front facings is different from a shirt with front bands.

Back Yoke for a Blouse with Front Facings

1. Stitch, turn, and press the collar.

2. Right sides together, stitch the front facing pieces to one yoke at the shoulder seams, matching the neck edges. Press seams toward the yoke. Set aside.

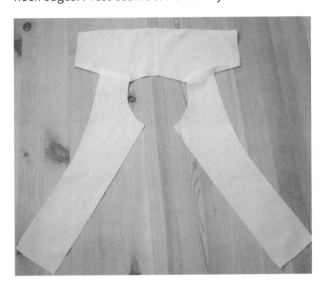

3. Right sides together, stitch the second yoke to the lower back, making a complete back piece.

4. Right sides together, sew the completed back to the garment front pieces at the shoulder seams. Press all the seams toward the yoke.

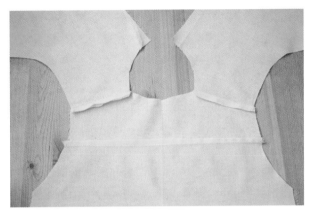

5. Baste the completed collar to the neck edge.

6. Right sides together, pin the yoke/facing unit to the garment, sandwiching the collar between the two units. Stitch up along the front, around the neckline, and down the other side. Grade (page 163), trim, and press seam allowances toward the body of the garment.

Close the Yoke by Machine

1. Turn the garment to the right side and press. From the right side, roll each side, the collar, and the back, into tight little "sausages." Lay these three sausages on the right side of the back yoke.

2. Pick up the inner yoke (the patterned fabric in the sample below) and wrap it around the sausages and over until you can line up the unsewn lower edge of this yoke with the bottom of the yoke stitched to the garment back. All sides should be right sides together. Pin the two yokes together and stitch over, or just inside, the previous stitching line.

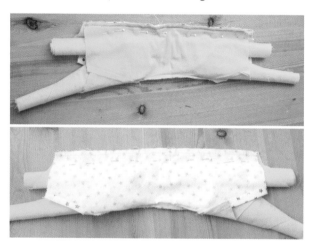

3. Reach into the yoke at each armhole opening and pull the fronts and back to the right side. Press. Topstitch along the yoke seams if you want. Such a neater inside finish than a back neck facing, with all the seams enclosed!

Finish the Shoulder Seams of the Inner Yoke

Although the yokes have been enclosed with the previous method, a little bit of the shoulder seam on the inner yoke will be open. You can reach in through the armhole and sew the shoulder seam and this little bit of yoke seam right sides together, as far as you can by machine, but I usually can't be bothered. Instead, I like to put my feet up, turn under this seam allowance, and hand stitch it to the shoulder seam, catching only a few threads with my needle.

Back Yoke for a Shirt with Front Bands

This is the method commonly used to "bag" the yoke of a tailored shirt before the collar band and collar are applied. Note that unlike the previous method, the two yokes are finally attached at the shoulder seams and not along the long bottom of the yoke.

1. Right sides together, stitch one yoke to the shirt back and to the shoulder seams of each front.

2. On the inside of the shirt sew the second yoke, right side of the yoke to the wrong side of shirt, along the back yoke stitching line, sandwiching the back between the two yokes. Trim and press all seam allowances up in the yoke. Topstitch if you want.

3. Flip the shirt over so you are working from the right side. Roll the back of the shirt and each of the fronts into tight "sausages" toward the shoulder seams, just as you would with the yoke treatment of a shirt with facings.

4. Wrap the remaining free unstitched shoulders of the yoke around this rolled up unit until they meet. Pin the shoulders of the two yokes together.

5. Stitch the shoulder seams through all layers, being careful not to catch any part of the fronts or back. Work from the outer yoke side and follow the previous stitching line.

6. Reach through the armholes and pull the shirt segments free one at a time. Press.

Chapter 3

Collars and Lapels

If collars were an Olympic diving event, I think most of us would give shirt collars and tailored lapels at least a 12 out of 10 in degree of difficulty. There is just that much that can go wrong. This is probably why we see these classic details increasingly absent from the pattern catalogs and indie offerings.

That's too bad. Most of us need shirts, coats, and jackets. The styles we choose shouldn't be constrained by fear.

It is completely possible to outsmart any difficulty in making collars and lapels. Completely. I have a menu of strategies for doing just that. Some of these methods involve reaching back to more traditional techniques. Some involve breaking down long, difficult seams into ones that are shorter and far more achievable. But whatever technique appeals to you, know each one of them is more ingenious than difficult, and more reliant on the wisdom of your hands than on excruciating precision.

Learning a new approach to a conventional task is often worth the effort. So often the easier way is the better way. And nothing makes a sewist feel more like an ace than turning out a beautiful collar. Who doesn't need to feel like that? It's not hard to get there.

EASY SHIRT COLLAR WITH A STAND

Yes, I know there are many ways to sew a shirt collar with a stand. I have tried them all, multiple times. I can't say most of these methods left me feeling particularly relaxed. So instead, whatever the instructions say, I use this chill method for great shirt collars. It works.

LOOK FAMILIAR?

The collar is off-center in the band. The distance from the end of the collar to the start of the band is a little different on each side. The shape of the curves at the end of the band is different too. There are also little bumps in the small area where the band meets the neckline and, as a result, the topstitching is slightly uneven. The end of the collar band doesn't line up with the edge of the front plackets, and oops, there is a bit of frayed fabric hanging out from a tiny unstitched section of one band/shirt intersection. The inner band, which as per instructions was not interfaced, was looser than the interfaced outer band and as a result some of that excess was caught in a tiny pleat in the topstitching. Pretty much a _F.A.I.L._ on many levels.

WHY THIS HAPPENS

The small but significant mistakes in this _F.A.I.L._ explain why so many sewists dread shirt collars. So much can go wrong in such a small but highly visible area. All these issues can be boiled down to three.

- There are many layers of fabric, and some interfacing, in a very restricted area. This makes it hard to topstitch evenly with changes in levels, even with devices like "hump jumpers." This also makes it extremely challenging to tuck up the band seam allowances into the band at that tricky front juncture.

- Much of the sewing is done blind, meaning the really important parts disappear under the presser foot just when you need to see them. You won't really know if everything is lined up neatly until later when the whole unit has been turned right side out.

- If you go off course at any point, it is really hard to correct mistakes. Unpicking the stitching at that crazy collar band / front placket / neckline intersection is more likely to lead to frayed nerves and fabric than a better result.

FIX IT RIGHT NOW

Hmm. Take the whole collar band and collar off and throw it in the corner. Then try the method below.

NEXT TIME

Interface Both Collar and Band

Fabric has life, stretch, and grain. Interfaced and non-interfaced pieces will behave differently. Interfacing both collar and stand pieces will give you the security of attaching like things to each other.

Since there will be double layers of interfacing in the collar and band, opt for a lighter weight of interfacing than you might use otherwise. Be sure to keep the interfacing out of the seam allowances. There are two ways to do this.

• **For a fusible interfacing:** Cut off all seam allowances before you fuse. I usually cut out the interfacing from the pattern pieces, then run a line of stitching a seam-allowance distance from the cut edges. I then trim to this stitching. So much easier than trying to measure and mark around the perimeter of a collar-shaped piece of interfacing!

• **For a sew-in interfacing:** Cut from the pattern, and loosely hand baste it to the wrong side of each fabric piece. After I sew the construction seams, I trim this interfacing right up the stitching in each seam allowance. Note how the corners have been clipped off to reduce bulk. With the space within that tight corner to be filled already with some seam allowances, I find removing this extra bit of interfacing at the corner really helpful.

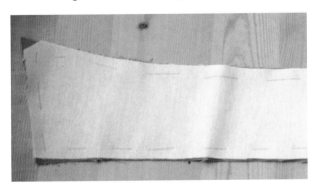

If you are allergic to hand basting, pin the interfacing to one wrong side of the two collar pieces before you stitch them together. The result will be the same.

Make the Collar

1. Stitch, trim out any woven interfacing from the seam allowances, turn, and press.

2. Stitch the two collar pieces together. Rather than stitching a hard pivot at the point, I walk a stitch or two (one for thinner fabrics, two or more for thicker fabrics) across the corners.

3. Trim bulk away from the corners in three distinct cuts—once across the point and then one angled up on each side, and grading the seam allowances (see Grade, page 163). Remember to leave the longer layer of seam allowance next to the upper collar to blend out the seam allowance bulk.

The interfacing is not shown in this sample so the stitches and trimming across the corner and the graded seam allowances are easier to see.

3. Turn and press. There are two tools I consider essential for collar pressing:

• A bamboo (not plastic) point turner for poking out the corners

• A point press for ironing those little seams

The bamboo turner does an excellent job of gently getting into corners without the risk of going through the fabric. The point press acts like a mini ironing board for pressing open the internal seams of the collar. If you don't have a point press handy, try a wooden rolling pin or the handle of a wood spoon—both have worked effectively for my students.

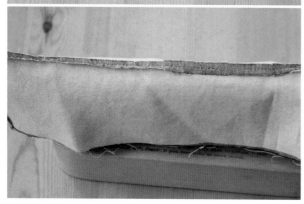

4. Once the collar has been turned and pressed properly—and this means rolling the seams under slightly to the back of the collar so they won't show on the right side—you will notice that the under-collar has slid forward, slightly past the cut edge of the upper collar.

Trim the two edges even before proceeding with construction. Baste the cut edges together if you like.

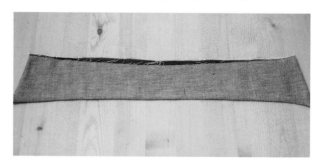

5. Topstitch around the collar. So that the stitches don't pack up at the corner, swing the other collar end under the back of the foot as a "hump jumper" to keep the foot level. It will be the perfect thickness. This little trick will save you from those tiny little stitches that sometimes occur when you just pivot and topstitch. If keeping your stitching straight is a challenge, try an edge-stitching foot for even stitches. See Tip: Accurate Topstitching (page 14).

Attach the Collar Bands

Sew the collar bands to the top of the shirt, sandwiching the body of the shirt in between them. Do this in two stages: Stitch one collar band on and then the other. Less stress.

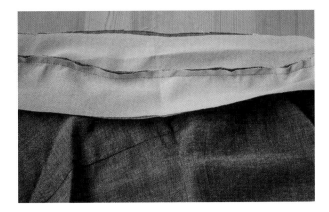

Sew the Ends of the Bands

Do this methodically, knowing there are many pause points for fine-tuning as you go.

1. Fold the front of the shirt out of the way a bit and pin.

2. Stitch each curved end of the band.

The object here is to get those curved ends stitched and to stop a comfortable distance before where the collar will need to be inserted. Just eyeball this. Any open area around the collar will be closed in the final topstitching.

Hints for stitching the curve:

• Use small stitches. Little steps always negotiate curves more smoothly.

• Backstitch near the garment edge but don't backstitch near the collar opening.

• Take it easy and check to make sure the stitching starts right at the button band (you should be able to feel it). You want that collar end to flow right into the shirt button bands. Relax and restitch until it is right. Notch the seam allowance (see Notch, page 163) to reduce bulk before you turn the band.

The stitching has started at the neck edge (the garment has been pinned out of the way) and has stopped just short of the opening for the collar.

At this point I would also press under the seam allowances of the collar opening in the bands.

Drop in the Collar

1. Slide the collar into the opening so the raw edge of the collar is even with the raw edge of the inside band, the one closest to your neck. It is really useful here if the opening is a little bigger than required. Unpick a few stitches in the band if necessary so the collar slips in easily.

2. Pin the collar to the inside band and stitch it in. Note it would probably be tricky to get the stitching right to the collar ends; don't worry about that. Any extra unstitched bits on the band will be caught later in the topstitching.

The upper collar and ends of the band as they appear from the inside neck edge of the shirt.

Hand Stitch the Outer Band to the Under-Collar

Fold under the seam allowance of the outer band (there should be a pressed line to follow as a guide) and slipstitch (page 168) it to the collar. Before you panic about my suggestion to do this step by hand, remember that this is not a lot of hand stitching, and it is under the collar. The nice thing about hand stitches is that you can take them out easily as you go, which cannot be said of machine stitches.

Take care not to pull the thread too tight when slipstitching, and the stitches will disappear during pressing.

Final Topstitching

Using an edge-stitching foot for accuracy and ease, topstitch all around the band, working with the inner collar and band facing you. This last stitching will close up any tiny openings around the collar.

COLLARS FOR HEAVY JACKET AND COATING FABRICS

LOOK FAMILIAR?

This jacket was made exactly by the pattern. Despite grading, trimming, and earnest pressing with a clapper and steam, this collar just looks lumpy and unprofessional. Note the big curve to the join between the lapel and collar.

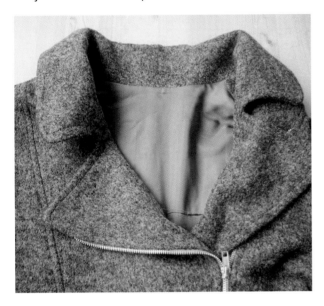

WHY THIS HAPPENS

Fabrics like the wools used in suits, jackets, and coats are often just too thick for conventional construction techniques. Multiple layers make the precision corners and edges of a tailored collar too difficult to sew with any reliability.

FIX IT RIGHT NOW

If you are brave—and at this point you might as well be—open this up and try again with one of the novel but effective methods described below.

NEXT TIME

Option 1: My Own Variation on the One-Giant-Seam Method

Suitable for lighter- to medium-weight fabrics, this modification of a popular method is successful because it takes into account stitching direction and turn of cloth, the internal volume that fabric will consume when turned to the right side.

As a rule, I am wary of any sewing operation that involves one giant seam of the up-one-side-across-and-down-the-other nature. In my experience, these mega-seams can be full of surprises when turned to the right side.

However, many patterns recommend exactly this method for attaching a jacket or coat collar. Typically, the advice is to sew the under-collar to the garment body and the upper collar to the facings, then attach both with a long seam pivoting at critical corners and joins. That, as per spec, was the method used to sew the _F.A.I.L._ In stitching and pivoting across multiple layers, the inner corner of the lapel collar join tends to freeze in lumps of fabric. No amount of clipping and trimming can quite eliminate it.

Follow these tips for a better result:

• Break up this long seam into manageable segments, stitching each part of each side in a similar direction so the grainline flow will be identical on both sides.

• Never cross another seam allowance and sew no more than two layers together at a time. This will mean some start-and-stop sewing as you move the seam allowances out of the way, but that's the secret to success.

• Respect the fact that a rolled collar needs room to roll. Leave a tiny hole without stitching right at that point where the collar joins the lapel. This gives the garment room to change direction, as required when the lapel and collar are turned to the right side, without puckering or pulling.

1. Prepare the under-collar. Stitch a center back seam if the pattern requires. This is often the case with a two-piece under-collar, each half cut on the bias. Interface and press-shape. At this point, I often pin the under-collar into a neckline shape on a tailor's ham, shoot it full of steam with an iron, and let it dry to help establish the roll line.

2. Staystitch the neck edge of the garment and clip (page 162) as often as necessary so the neckline can be pulled into a straight line.

3. Pin and stitch the under-collar to the garment in two steps, from each end of the collar piece (or from the dot on the pattern piece, depending on the style) to the center back. This is directional stitching, the same as the staystitching, and works with the grain.

Also, it is easier to start right at a crucial point than to try and end at it once things are traveling under the presser foot.

You may find the collar seems larger than the neck edge and is a bit of a struggle to fit in. Make more clips in the seam allowances, right to the staystitching, to help that garment edge open up enough to fit the collar comfortably.

Trim and press this seam open over a seam roll. The seam roll will allow you to isolate the seamline as you press, keeping the shaped facings and garment from catching under the iron and creasing.

4. Sew the back neck facing (or in some cases the back lining piece) to each facing at the shoulders.

5. Sew the upper collar to the facing unit, again in two steps, from a point a seam-allowance distance from each end of the collar piece (or the dot marking on the pattern piece) to the center back.

6. Pin the facing / upper collar unit to the garment / lower collar unit all around the edges—long facings to fronts, tops of lapels, and around the two collar edges.

7. Stitch the lapels of the garment in two seams, one on each side. First, moving all seam allowances out of the way, drop the needle down at the collar/lapel join dot. Rather than backstitching here, change to a very short stitch length for the first little bit. This will be easier to take out if necessary.

Stitch from here across to the point of the lapel, pivot, take two stitches diagonally across the corner of the lapel, pivot, sew down about 2″ (5cm), then change to a usual stitch length and complete the seam right to the hem.

Stitching no more than two layers at a time will prevent those funny lumps at the lapel corner and, since none of the seam allowances are trapped, will allow the collar and lapel to turn to the right side naturally.

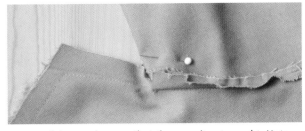

8. Repeat on the other side.

I have pinned some of the bulk of the garment and seam allowances out of the way here so that they won't get caught. Note how the lapel stitching line stops short of the point where the collar stitching starts. This little space is wonderful, so don't worry about it. If you ever decide you want to make this gap smaller, you can always add a hand stitch or two later.

9. Stitch the collars together, again in two steps. Once more, move all the seam allowances out of the way and drop the needle down at the collar/lapel join. But don't try to meet the previous stitching exactly. Instead, give yourself a couple of stitches of space to create that tiny hole the collar needs for mobility and roll. Using a smaller-than-usual stitch length (about 1.5), stitch up to the corner of the collar, pivot, take two stitches diagonally across the corner, pivot, and sew to the center back of the collar. Do exactly the same thing, sewing in the same direction up the collar and to the center back, on the other side.

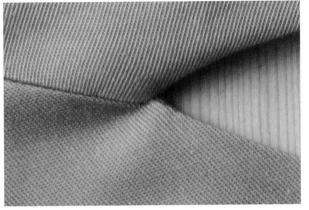

The join here is smooth and thin as seen from the underside of the lapel join.

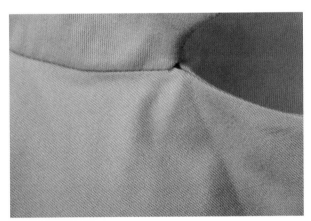

Bird's eye view of the four seams at the collar/lapel join. The tiny hole at this intersection can be seen but really is otherwise not apparent at all.

10. Trim, grade (page 163), and press. Working from the inside of the garment, loosely hand stitch the upper and lower collar seam allowances together at the neck edge. To ensure the mobility of the fabric layers necessary to get a nice roll, it is important that the two collars have not been machine stitched together and that the hand stitches used now to join them are a bit loose.

11. Topstitch the lapel (see How to Topstitch the Lapel, page 51).

Option 2: The Brilliant Menswear "Felt Under-Collar" Method

This option—actually my favorite, because it provides a lot of room for tiny adjustments to perfection before any final stitching—is a menswear technique and suitable for medium to heavy fabric. My version is a bit of a hybrid. I use both the trimmed under-collar of menswear tailoring and the facing and collar unit of the One Giant Seam advised in many women's patterns.

To understand tailored collars, it makes sense to study the work of those who have made most of them—the tailors of men's suits. Tailors actually have a relaxed and effective approach to collar making. They line up the layers, position them so they look right, and then sew them down. When you make a collar this way, it feels more like a process of arranging layers rather than a process of much stitching and turning, such as described in Option 1: My Own Variation on the One-Giant-Seam Method (page 45).

Here is what the under-collar of a tailor-made suit looks like.

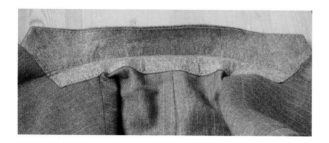

This approach is so easy it will make you cry. I mean it. Finish the neck edge, press under the seam allowances of the upper collar, stitch that collar to the garment, and then just hand stitch down a felted under-collar. Note that this technique requires a pattern with a back neck facing and/or lining.

All the work is done from the right side, with many pause points to make sure everything is positioned exactly where it should be. I find this method works really well when using felted wool flannel for the under-collar. It is easy to make felted wool by washing and drying fashion wool at high temperatures. This method is also suitable for jackets or coats with a velvet upper collar faced by a nonfraying under-collar. Those velvet collars are pretty sharp; I look forward to when they are back in style. The process is different, but easy.

Yes, I know this technique requires a lot of little hand stitches, and some folks might be wary of that, but think of the payoff. And the absence of a seam ripper

in this process. If you still have doubts about hand stitching, I have one word for you: Netflix. The results of a little quiet hand sewing are worth it.

1. Make or choose a nonfraying under-collar piece. This fabric also needs to be lighter or, if working with a relatively thin fabric, no thicker than the fashion fabric. Be creative. For very heavy fabrics, such as the boiled wool used in the *F.A.I.L.* garment, a synthetic suede can be a practical choice.

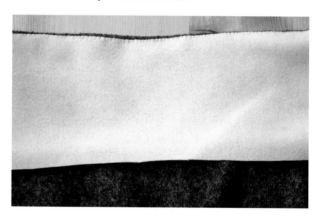

For the sample that follows, I washed and dried some of the wool flannel of my jacket at a high heat in the washer and dryer to make my felted under-collar. Note this piece will be well attached by tiny hand felling stitches that will contain the cut edges pretty well. The object of the felting process is just to mat the fibers together a bit to help the process along—no need to worry about making it completely nonraveling.

2. Trim the sides and top seam allowances from the under-collar piece. Remove all but ¼″ (0.5cm) of the neckline seam allowance.

3. Prepare the upper collar. Interface and press under the top and side seam allowances.

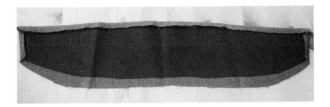

Trim these seam allowances to ¼″ (0.5cm). Leave the neckline seam allowance intact.

It will probably be necessary to remove a little fabric at the corners to reduce bulk. I generally pinch out the two corner seam allowances and clip a bit off. Be careful not to clip too close to the corner, however, as you want to keep those corners neat without fraying.

Check to make sure the two sides of the collar are exactly the same height after trimming. It is also important to turn the collar over and admire how it looks, particularly the ends—thin and flat and beautiful. It is pretty hard to get this degree of smooth precision with any other method of tailoring a collar.

4. Stitch the front facings to the back neck facing. In some patterns this will be the back lining rather than a back neck facing.

5. Stitch the upper collar to the facings unit, as in Option 1: My Own Variation on the One-Giant-Seam Method, Step 5 (page 45).

6. Stitch the facing/upper collar unit to the garment. Tuck the upper collar down and out of the way and stitch the facing to the garment in, you guessed it, one large seam. For accuracy and to make sure the two sides turn out even, stitch this seam in two steps—from center back down and around the lapel to the hem.

7. Grade (page 163) the seam allowances, clip the lapel corners, turn, and press. Note the one-giant-seam approach works here because the bulk of the extra seams of the under-collar are absent. Huge, huge difference. Notice how nice and sharp the inside corners of the lapel/collar are. Like me, haven't you spent years wishing you could get your collars to look like this?

8. Working from the outside back of the garment, pin the trimmed under-collar to the upper collar. Confirm that the bottom edge covers the stitching used to attach the upper collar to the garment and that all other edges lie just in from the folded edges of the collar. Try rolling the collar in your hands, making sure it fits nicely. If necessary, trim the edges of the under-collar to fit.

9. Hand stitch each side of the under-collar to the neck edge and upper collar with a fell stitch, short, closely spaced vertical stitches (see Fell or Felling Stitch, page 166).

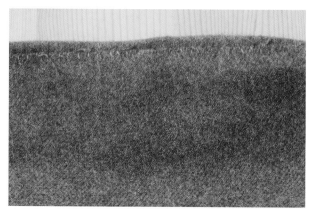

The under-collar fell stitched to cover the folded seam allowances of the upper collar and cover the neckline seam.

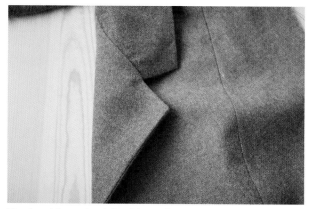

The lapel from the right side. Unfortunately, you can't reach through this book and feel how thin the edges of the collar and lapel feel with that extra seam allowance bulk missing.

10. Loosely hand stitch the neck seams of both collars together, working from inside the garment just like you did in Option 1: My Own Variation on the One-Giant-Seam Method (page 45).

11. Topstitch the lapel (see How to Topstitch the Lapel, next page).

How to Topstitch the Lapel

Whatever option you choose to sew the lapel, the last stage is to topstitch around all edges.

At this point, the temptation is to just topstitch up the facing, pivot onto the collar, stitch around the collar, pivot, and stitch down the remaining facing. A blouse is topstitched this way.

The circumstances of sewing through tailoring fabrics requires a sneaky addition to this approach—an almost invisible short line of topstitching that is buried in the well of the seam to transition between the collar and neckline. This super-important segment of stitching flattens the layers of fabric in that joint and is critical to articulating the proper angle of the lapel.

Here are the topstitching steps done in four pivots per lapel. I want you to know that I wouldn't actually topstitch a nice gray wool flannel with heavy yellow thread, but I felt there was some educational value in doing this.

- **Pivot 1:** Stitch up the facing. Needle down, presser foot up, and pivot at the corner of the lapel.

- **Pivot 2:** Stitch along the top of the lapel until you are even with the end of the collar stop. Needle down parallel to the collar edge, presser foot up, pivot, and sew right up to the neck seam.

- **Pivot 3:** At the neck seam, needle down and presser foot up, pivot, and sew in-the-ditch of the neckline seam up to the topstitching width from the edge of the collar. You can see these 2–3 stitches slightly here. If you use matching thread and take care to spread the fabric slightly on either side of the seam, your stitches will disappear.

- **Pivot 4:** Needle down, presser foot up, pivot, and topstitch around the collar.

- Reverse the process as you topstitch toward the remaining lapel.

Chapter 4

Plackets, Tabs, Yoke Inserts, and V-Necklines

Let's just say it. Corners around necklines can be hard. Whether they are at the turning point of a V, at the bottom of a placket or yoke, or on a tab front, these small areas of intersection can ruin your day and your garment.

To conquer these details, consider that instructions for these tricky corners might be the problem, not you. If you can get your head around that, it is easier to come up with a strategy to deal with the issues before they happen.

You can start by questioning the number of pattern pieces. In my experience, it is so often easier to use a "big piece of fabric" and trim it to fit as you go along rather than try to exert precision on small units.

It's also helpful to work from the right side and with your hands whenever you can. Smooth the fabric where it needs to be, trim off any excess, and then use stitching to confirm the arrangement. It's as simple as that.

All the details in this chapter—crossover and mitered V's, tab fronts, and yoke inserts—are constructed according to these principles. I think you will find all these necklines surprisingly easy to sew.

SHARP CORNERS IN YOKES

There are many internal corners in garments, but the most obvious are set-in yokes. I classify these details as "looks easy, is hard" and am mystified why so many "easy" patterns include them. The way to get on top of the corner situation is to deconstruct the whole process. Break down one long, ambitious seam into several shorter ones, and make sure these seams are sewn in the same direction.

LOOK FAMILIAR?

I love the lines of this vintage top pattern. The long darts create angles in the garment meant to be mirrored by the point of the yoke insert—a sharp design idea. However, in execution, this one is a _F.A.I.L._ Fabric has been caught up in the pivot, a bit of the staystitching shows, and there is a weird bubble right where there should be a clean point.

WHY THIS HAPPENS

The instructions for this corner, as in most patterns, are to staystitch, clip, sew down one side of the yoke to the clip, pivot, and sew back up the second side of the yoke. This can be really hard to do when the most important sections disappear and catch under the presser foot. Also, sewing such a precise area in different directions, down one side and up the other, has the effect of pushing the grain down to a point where it has nowhere to go, and then twisting the grain during the pivot, almost guaranteeing a bubble like the one above.

FIX IT RIGHT NOW

The more redos you try, the worse it gets. If it was me, and I was feeling determined, I would remove the yoke and do my best to press the neckline flat. Then I would cut out a new yoke, press under the seam allowances, lay it on top of garment, and topstitch it down. This applique approach wouldn't be quite as elegant as a proper insert yoke, but it would look better than the _F.A.I.L._ here.

NEXT TIME

Before we go further, we must discuss two important principles:

- **Principle 1:** Cross seams don't pivot. Sew each of these crossing seams away from the corner, rather than into it. Directional sewing will keep the grain moving out of the corner, rather than into it where it might pool in a little bubble.

- **Principle 2:** Clip to the stitch; don't try to stitch to the clip. When an angled piece is inserted into a garment, the seam allowances need to be clipped so they will open up enough to fit the new piece. Making stitches land right on the edge of a clip is hard. Clipping right to the stitches after they have been made is easy. You have so much more control when you can see what you are doing.

In practice, this is how those principles would be applied to inserting the corners of a yoke in a woven fabric.

1. Instead of staystitching, place a small square of lightweight knit fusible interfacing right over the point of the V, where you will need to clip. The interfacing will keep the clip from fraying or stretching without the eventual risk of staystitch show-through.

2. Mark the spot just below the point of the V where the two seams will intersect.

3. Pin one side of the insert to the garment seam. Working from the wrong side—where you can see the marked point drawn over the interfacing square—lower the needle right on the mark and sew up and away from this point. Then clip through the garment fabric only, right to the first stitch at the marked point.

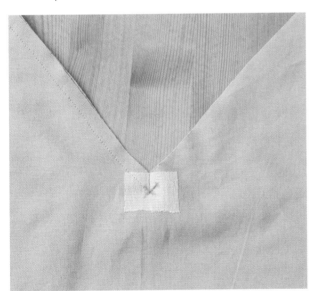

4. Straightening out the fabric (which is now possible because the area has been clipped), sew the second side of yoke, again stitching away from the corner, not into it. Remember the objective here is to cross seams, so don't worry if you start a stitch or two before the point of intersection.

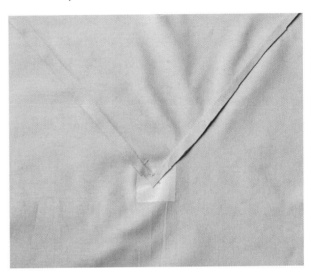

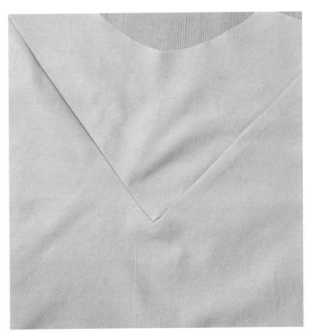

5. Trim and finish the seam allowances and press.

V-NECKLINES IN KNITS

I think V-necklines suit most people. Garments with these necklines are comfortable and easy to get on and off. I like to put V-necks in T-shirts, in children's clothes, and in nightwear. I even add knit V-necklines to flannel night shirts. However, not all V-neckline techniques are easy or give predictable results. So, I am careful to use only two low-stress methods—one for a mitered V and one without—that rely on my eyes and hands rather than formulas or tricky techniques.

LOOK FAMILIAR?

A good try with a mitered V here, but also a bit of a disappointment and a *F.A.I.L.* There is a lot of bulk behind this miter, creating a dimple below the point of the V. And I regret to note that the sides of the band on either side of the V don't quite meet up.

The wrong side of this neckline says a lot. The popular method of applying the band leaves a lot of bulk right where this neckline needs to lie flat.

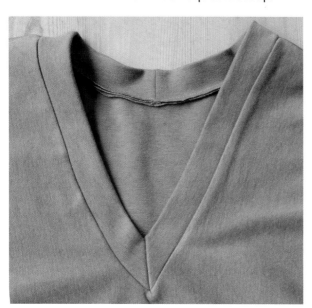

WHY THIS HAPPENS

I think this technique, one often suggested in patterns, means well. The idea of just inserting a band and zipping a small dart up at center front seems so easy. In fact, this is a technique I suggested as a fix for a baggy band in Chapter 1: Neckbands and Binding (page 8). But this way of finishing a V-neck is an emergency technique only. The little dart in the band can add fabric bulk right at center front, and accurate stitching through a knit band can be difficult. The *F.A.I.L.* above is not unusual with this technique.

FIX IT RIGHT NOW

I might wear a scarf or necklace with this top and decide slight imperfections don't matter. Alternately, you could remove the band and apply a crossover V (next page) or encased miter band (page 59) instead.

NEXT TIME

Crossover V

Of the two V-neckline techniques included here, the crossover V is definitely the most foolproof. It is also a style of V-neckline that can be added to any knit top for a variety of uses. Deep V's make great vests or pullovers, and more modest V's can easily be used to convert a standard crew neck tee to a V.

The trick with this technique is that so much of it is done with your hands before you commit to any stitching. In addition, there are a number of pause points at which it is easy to stop and adjust to fix any issues. *Note:* For a woman's garment, the V goes right to left, so the gap in the stitching is on the left side. For a man's garment, this is reversed. (Thank you for not asking me why.)

CUT OUT THE BAND AND PREPARE THE GARMENT

1. Establish the length of the neckband.

A. Measure up each side of the V to the shoulder seam and multiply by 2.

B. Measure around the back of the neckline from shoulder seam to shoulder seam and subtract about 25%. Having the neckband a little shorter at the back neck means it will be stretched when stitched and hug the neck in a little. You want this.

A + B = neckband length to cut. To this measurement, add at least 3˝ (8cm) in length so your hands will have something to hold on to.

2. Establish the width of the neckband.

Work out your preferred band width and multiply by 2, since the band will be folded, then add two seam allowances.

3. Reinforce the point of the V on the wrong side of the garment by ironing on a small square of fusible knit interfacing. This is an alternative to staystitching, which patterns often suggest.

4. Sew the front and back of the garment together at the shoulder seams.

SEW THE BAND

1. Fold the band in half lengthwise, wrong sides together. Pin it to the right side of the neckline (assuming this top is for a woman). Lay the band flat without stretching along the sides of the V, but stretch it slightly across the back of the neck between the two shoulder seams. Pin to the left side of the neckline, not stretching the band at all. Make sure you leave a good bit of band free at the bottom of the V for handling later on. Any excess can be trimmed.

2. Sew up one side of the band, starting at the point that is a seam-allowance distance directly below the V. Stitch across the back neck, stretching the band slightly to achieve that slight cup to the neck, and down the other side. Stop stitching a distance from the bottom of the V, that is at least equal to the width of the folded band plus some comfortable extra. I usually add about 1˝ (2.5cm) to the band-width measurement in calculating where to stop stitching.

Tip **Stretch Protection for the Neck Band**

Because there is little stress on this open neckline, it is fine to sew the band on with a straight stitch. If you would still like some stretch protection for the knit fabric, sew with either a tiny zigzag or with a straight stitch but with wooly nylon thread hand wound in the bobbin.

3. Clip through the garment fabric only to the point at the bottom of the V, right where the line of stitching started.

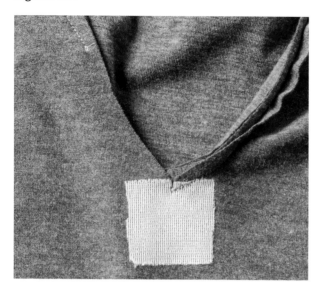

ARRANGE THE BAND

Take a breath. It gets easier now.

1. Turn the garment to the right side and think about how you want this neckline to look.

2. Tuck under the open seam allowance on the side you left open on the left. Using your hands and taking your time, arrange the remaining left end of the band under the first/right side of the band. Use pins to secure.

One pin secures the crossed ends of the band over each other. The remaining pins secure the tucked-under seam allowance.

FINISH STITCHING THE BAND

1. Turn the garment to the inside and stitch the small gap in the previous stitching closed. Try to end the stitching close to the previous stitches and not beyond them, as in the green stitches below.

2. Again working from the inside, sew the free end of the remaining band to the opposite seam allowance. See the short line of green stitching here too.

3. Trim away any excess band length and, if you want, finish the seam allowances with a small zigzag stitch.

The Encased Mitered V

This method is slightly more complex than the crossover V. But since the seams of the miter are hidden inside the band, I think this is a nicer approach than the faux miter used to make the *F.A.I.L.* neckline.

PREPARE THE NECKLINE

1. Sew the garment shoulder seams.

2. Iron a small piece of fusible knit interfacing to the wrong side of the fabric below the point of the V.

3. Mark a point a seam allowance distance away and directly below the point of the V on this interfaced patch.

4. Establish the length of the neckband:

  A. Measure up each side of the V to the shoulder seam and multiply by 2.

  B. Measure around the back of the neckline from shoulder seam to shoulder seam and subtract about 25%. Having the neckband a little shorter at the back neck means it will be stretched when stitched and hung the neck in a little. You want this.

Add A + B + 2 seam allowances = neckband length to cut.

5. Establish the width of the neckband. Cut the band the finished width times 2 as it will be folded, plus 2 seam allowances.

DEFINE THE MITER

Take it slow, this is easier than it seems.

1. Fold the front of the garment in half lengthwise along center front, right sides together. Don't fold the bands in half; the miter is drawn in single layers before the two ends are stitched together.

2. Lay one end of the neckband, wrong side of the fabric facing you, raw edges even with the raw edge of the neckline and the corner of the short edge of the band exactly at the point of the V.

3. Line up a ruler right along the fold line and up into the band area; I know this all seems weird but stay with me. Using the ruler as a guide, draw a line on the band, continuing the angle of the fold through to the edge of the band.

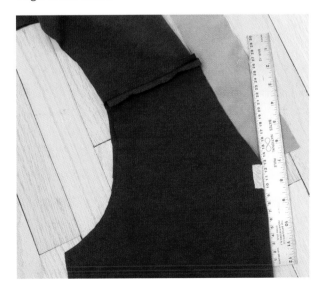

4. Use the ruler to draw a line from the opposite short corner to the point directly opposite of where the first line ran off the edge of the band. This little maneuver, working from the angle of the neckline itself to determine a customized angle of the miter, is far more accurate than any geometric formula.

You will have drawn a little V-shape at the end of the band. These lines are the stitching lines of the miter! I love things that work even if I don't exactly understand them.

5. Right sides together, lay the end of the marked band over the other end of the band, pin, and stitch

through both layers along the marked lines, pivoting where the lines intersect. Trim away the excess fabric from below the V of stitching, and clip to the point. Gently press the seams open.

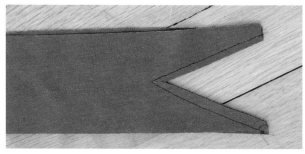

6. Fold the stitched band in half and surprise—a miter. Baste the raw edges of the band together.

APPLY THE BAND

1. Pin one side of the band to the neckline, right sides together. Make sure that the seamline of the miter lies directly over the mark indicating the seam allowance distance below the point of the V.

2. Lower the needle exactly at the seam that defines the miter and stitch up one side, around the back neck, stretching the band slightly to fit, and down the second side to end right at the same spot in the miter. I usually pause during this run of stitching, somewhere around the first shoulder seam, and clip through the garment fabric, not the band, at the point of the V right to that first stitch. I do this because it is always, always easier to clip to the stitch than it is to stitch to the clip. See my note about this in Sharp Corners in Yokes (page 54). Turn the garment

to the right side and press lightly. I always use a pressing cloth to prevent shine on the fabric.

3. Finish the seam with a small zigzag stitch or on the serger. Topstitch if you want to, but use hand wound wooly nylon in the bobbin for some added stretch to the seam.

TAB FRONT NECKLINES

Tab front necklines are a classic. They can be made in knit fabrics, or in rugby-shirt wovens sewn onto knit garments. Tab necklines traditionally have been used in golf shirts and those nice, preppy tab-front knit dresses. These necklines also have facings that extend and wrap around a collar. The tabs themselves overlap and close the neckline below the collar. They are usually finished with buttons or snaps.

As a general rule, the tab width for children's garments is 1″ (2.5cm), for women 1½″ (4cm), and for men 1½″–2″ (4–5cm).

LOOK FAMILIAR?

I am sorry to say this tab front turned out to be a *F.A.I.L.* The sides of the tab were fine, but of different widths, the stitching at the bottom of the tab is less than accurate, and the tabs don't line up perfectly.

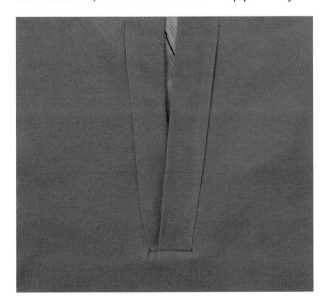

FIX IT RIGHT NOW

I hope the bottom area of this band has been reinforced on the wrong side with some fusible knit interfacing, rather than staystitching. That alone will make it easier to unpick the stitches around the bottom "box" of the bands. If you were able to unstitch, then follow the instructions that follow for arranging the bands from the right side. Alternately, you can remove both tabs and redo the neckline with a woven, rather than knit tab. The woven fabric tabs will be more stable than knit fabric and this will be helpful when dealing the second time around with tired knit edges.

Finally, and this is probably the most desperate solution (so, of course, one I have used myself), you can make a small rectangular patch out of a sporty ribbon and sew it over the messy bottom of the tab. To make this rescue look intentional, try to find some other place in the garment to use this same ribbon—on a pocket, to face the hem, or even to tape the back of the neckline.

NEXT TIME

Visible Tabs

Very often, patterns for visible tabs have a rectangular box cut right out of the garment fabric into which the tab pieces must be very accurately inserted. This was the method used to make the *F.A.I.L.* here. The problem with this approach is that the sewist is left to negotiate tiny seams in stretchy fabric and often instructed to do some of the sewing blind from the wrong side. The method I use, with less stress, dispenses with fussy markings and measuring, relies on arranging the shapes with your hands before committing them to stitching, and doesn't cut into the garment until the stitching is done.

SET UP THE TAB FOR STITCHING

1. Your pattern may come with a pattern piece for the tab/facings, or you can make your own. When I don't have a pattern piece to work with, or when I want to add a tab to a plain T-shirt pattern, I generally just pin a sizable piece of fabric to the front of the garment, stitch the tab, and then turn and trim this fabric into a facing shape on the wrong side later. If you do this, or if you use the provided pattern pieces, the first step in construction is make a paper stitching template the width and length of the finished tab.

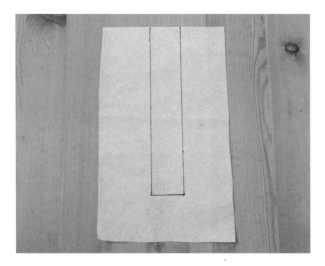

2. Fold the garment front right sides together in half and lightly press a fold line along center front.

3. Lay the facing pieces cut sides even with the pressed center front line, right sides together, and pin. Alternately, lay a single rectangle of fabric over the garment, right sides together, with the piece extending about 2″ (5cm) above the shoulder.

4. Pin the paper tab template centered below the neckline over the two layers of fabric.

STITCH THE TAB SIDES

1. Stitch the sides only of the tab box. Use a small stitch length and do not backstitch. The paper will stabilize the stitching. Remove the paper after stitching.

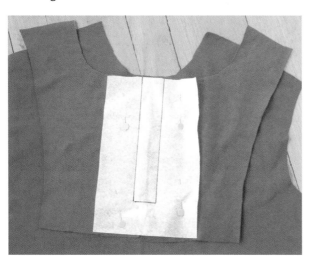

2. Cut two rectangles of fuse-on interfacing to the measurement of the tab box / finished tab dimension. Fuse a rectangle to each side of the tab fabric, flush with the stitching line. Yes, I know it seems crazy to add the interfacing at this point, but doing so now positions it very accurately next to the stitching line.

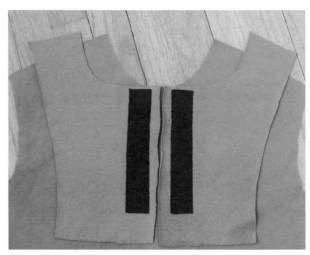

3. Cut between the stitching lines in the garment fabric but stop the cut about 1″ (2.5cm) from the bottom of the stitching. Make diagonal cuts to that last stitch on each side, through the garment fabric only.

4. Trim the inside of the tab box seam allowances to ¼″ (0.5cm). Be careful to leave the wedge shape at the bottom intact. Press these seam allowances gently toward the tabs.

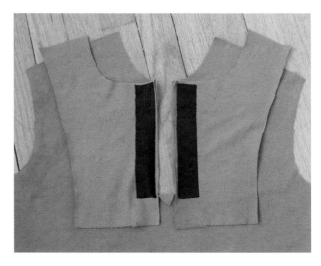

ARRANGE THE TABS

1. Working from the right side, fold each tab and lay them over each other. Right to left for women, left to right for men.

Fool around with the tabs to make sure they are the same width all the way up, that they fill the tab box, and that the two tabs are lying exactly on top of each other. I always find it easiest to work with just one tab at a time, folding it under, measuring, pinning, and then pressing once I have it right.

2. When you are satisfied with your arrangement, pin the tabs together and in place. Next, tuck the ends into the unstitched area at the bottom of the box. If there are any puckers, double-check that the clips to the corner have gone all the way to that last stitch.

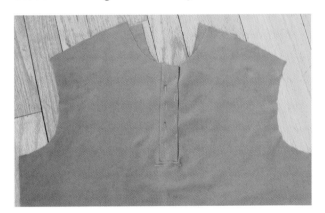

3. Working from the inside, flip the garment up to expose the cut wedge and ends of the tabs. Fold the garment in an even fold. Measure from each side of the fold to the hem to confirm that the fold is square at the bottom of the tab.

4. Hand or machine baste a short seam through all layers and check on the right side that the bottom of the tab box is level. When you are satisfied, machine stitch to close the tab box. I often use a zipper foot to do this.

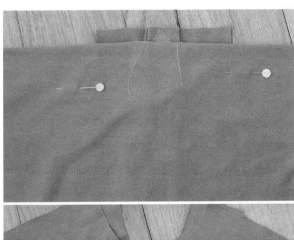

5. If you are working with one large piece of facing fabric rather than facing pattern pieces, trim the facing to match the neck edge, following along the shoulder line for 2˝ (5cm) and then down to below the tabs on the inside in a nice curve.

FINISH THE COLLAR

1. Sew the shoulder seams and press.

2. Pin a completed collar to the neck edge, ends of collar at center front, in the middle of the tabs. Baste in place.

3. Wrap the top edges of the facings around the collar. Pin and stitch.

FINISHING THE BACK SEAM

A serged seam might be all you want to finish the back neck. Alternately, you may decide to cover the seam allowance with a woven twill tape as is often done in ready-to-wear or with a fabric tape you have made yourself.

1. Lay the tape over the neckline seam allowance, butted right up next to the stitching line, stopping about 1″ (2.5cm) in under the facing,

2. Stitch the tape to the seam allowance as close as you can to the collar/neckline stitching line.

3. Turn the facings to the right side and press. Top-stitch the tape/binding to the back neck edge from a little past each shoulder seam.

OPTIONAL TOPSTITCHING

A small box is often topstitched at the bottom of tabs made with woven fabric. When working with knit fabrics, I usually rely on buttons and buttonholes to hold the tabs in place instead. You can also stitch-in-the-ditch (burying the machine stitches in the well of the seams) around the tab if you'd like to. I have done that stitching here with a darker thread so you can just see it.

Tip Sleeve Placket—Just an Upside-Down Tab

Many woven dresses and tunics call for a longer version of a tab front. The pattern pieces and instructions for these can be elaborate, and challenging. Once when putting away my husband's shirts, I noticed that a standard very easy-to-sew Tailored Sleeve Placket (page 111) is just another kind of tab front, just upside down! Try the same technique used in sleeves for your next woven fabric tab front.

Hidden Plackets

Although a neckline with visible tabs is traditional, a tab hidden behind the placket opening is seen more often these days in golf shirts and other polo style tops and dresses. This treatment is frequently combined with premade knit collars and taped-back necklines.

Like the conventional tab, I often cut my own placket shape, do my markings on paper I can stitch through, use a fusible interfacing in lieu of staystitching, and minimize topstitching, particularly when working with stretchy knits.

It's helpful to understand the differences between this and the conventional tab front. Unlike the tab, the hidden placket in this style of polo is made from just one piece of fabric. The opening is made with an offset stitching/slash line, with the larger portion of the fabric to the left for women, to the right for men. This larger side of the fabric is used to make the one hidden tab. The other side is a simple facing for the placket opening. It is important to remember that the actual cut and faced opening for this neckline is not at center front but lays over to cover the outer edge of the hidden placket. Buttons or snaps, however, are lined up right along the centerline.

These hidden plackets are fun to make, just keep it slow. And remember to breathe.

CUT AND INTERFACE THE PLACKET PIECE

If you are using a pattern for this type of neckline, the pattern piece for the placket will be provided. Unlike the traditional tab, where tab width and length tend to be different for men, women, and children, hidden plackets are generally 1″ (2.5cm) wide and about 6″ (15cm) long for adults and about 3½″ (9cm) long for children.

PREP THE FRONT AND PLACKET PIECE

1. Fold the garment front in half lengthwise, right sides together, and press to mark the center front. Do the same with the facing/tab piece.

2. Interface and then press under the ¼″ (0.5cm) seam allowances along each long side of the facing/tab piece.

3. Make a paper stitching template by tracing just the marked stitching lines and the center front from the facing pattern piece.

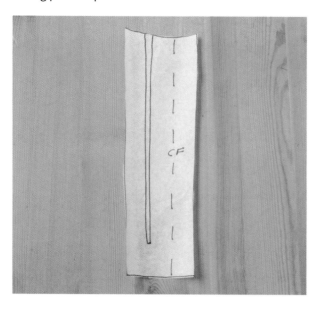

4. Pin the placket piece to the garment front, right sides together and carefully lining up the pressing marks for center front. Lay the paper template over these two layers, making sure that the marked center front line is right over the pressing marks for center front.

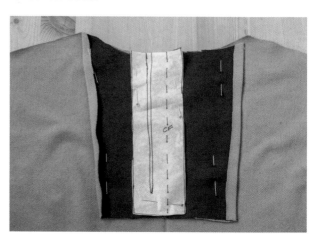

STITCH THE PLACKET OPENING

1. Working from the right side, stitch through the paper down to the bottom as marked.

2. Pivot and hand turn two stitches, pivot again, and stitch up to the neckline. Make sure you leave just enough space between the two lines to cut the fabric between them. If not, restitch.

3. Slash down the opening right to the bottom stitches. Put a pin across the bottom of the slash so you don't cut through those last stitches.

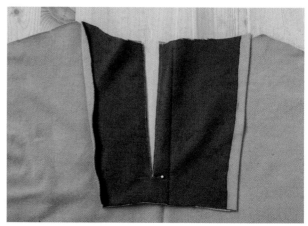

Notice how the slash opening is offset from the center front, marked with the press lines.

FORM THE PLACKET

1. Pull the facing/tab piece through to the wrong side and press the opening lightly and neatly, turning the facing to the wrong side on the stitching line on the faced, not tab side. For here that would be the right for a woman's shirt.

2. Working from the right side, fold the larger portion of the placket fabric (left for women, right for men) so the stitched edge is even with the slashed opening, forming the hidden tab. Check to make sure the tab is the same consistent width, usually 1″ (2.5cm) wide. Pin and press lightly.

COMPLETE THE PLACKET

1. Sew the shoulder seams and attach and finish the collar with the same technique used for the traditional tab neckline.

2. Turn the tab and facings and lightly press the completed placket.

3. Sew the bottom of the facing and tab together but note that this is more an attachment job, rather than forming the bottom of the stitching box as in the traditional tab front. There is no need to get stressed about getting this stitching very close.

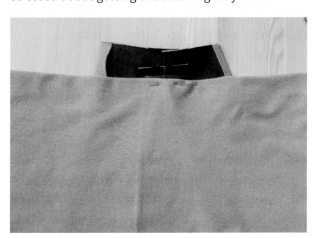

I usually keep topstitching very simple, as there is always a risk with knit fabrics of distorting the shape with too much stitching. You may notice that in ready-to-wear, the tab edges and the outline of the facing are often topstitched, as well as an X-shape at the bottom of the tab.

I generally do two short parallel rows of stitching just below the bottom of the placket opening. I count on buttons and buttonholes to mostly hold the placket edges. I also stitch-in-the-ditch (in the well) of the tab seam. If you find the ditch stitching stressful, you can just stitch an even distance from the seamline instead. I did that here.

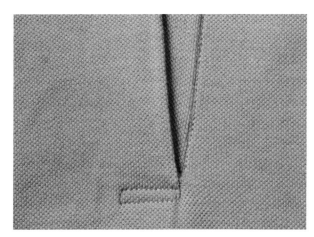

Chapter 5

Pockets

We all need pockets. Sometimes I am in a sewing hurry and eliminate them. I then spend the rest of my time reaching for where they should be.

So why don't I put those pockets in? Good question. My suspicion is that the stressless sewists among us, like myself, find them picky and tricky.

The so-called inseam pockets tend to float around. Sometimes they pull out of the opening, or worst of all, add bulk at hip height. Small pockets, like the little ones for cell phones, are useful but can be time-consuming to make. Even large patch pockets in heavy fabrics, so useful for hand warming, can be difficult to execute professionally. And the welt pocket family—single, double, and flapped—make for elegant pockets but can be complicated to sew and involve a slot cut right through the garment to make them. Not many of us look forward to doing that.

But we still need pockets. We need them for phones, for keys, for credit cards, and for a quick run to the store. We need them for little bags when we walk the dog and for tissues to wipe the baby's nose. We need pockets because life needs stuff, and pockets are where we put it. One of my oldest vintage sewing texts says that every well-dressed man should have at least 20 pockets in his complete outfit! Pockets are necessary.

So, to make the pockets without angst, I have worked up a few systems that make them easy to add to any garment. All these methods involve doing more with less. All of them are the only pocket techniques I use. See what you think. I hope you will find your new pockets handy.

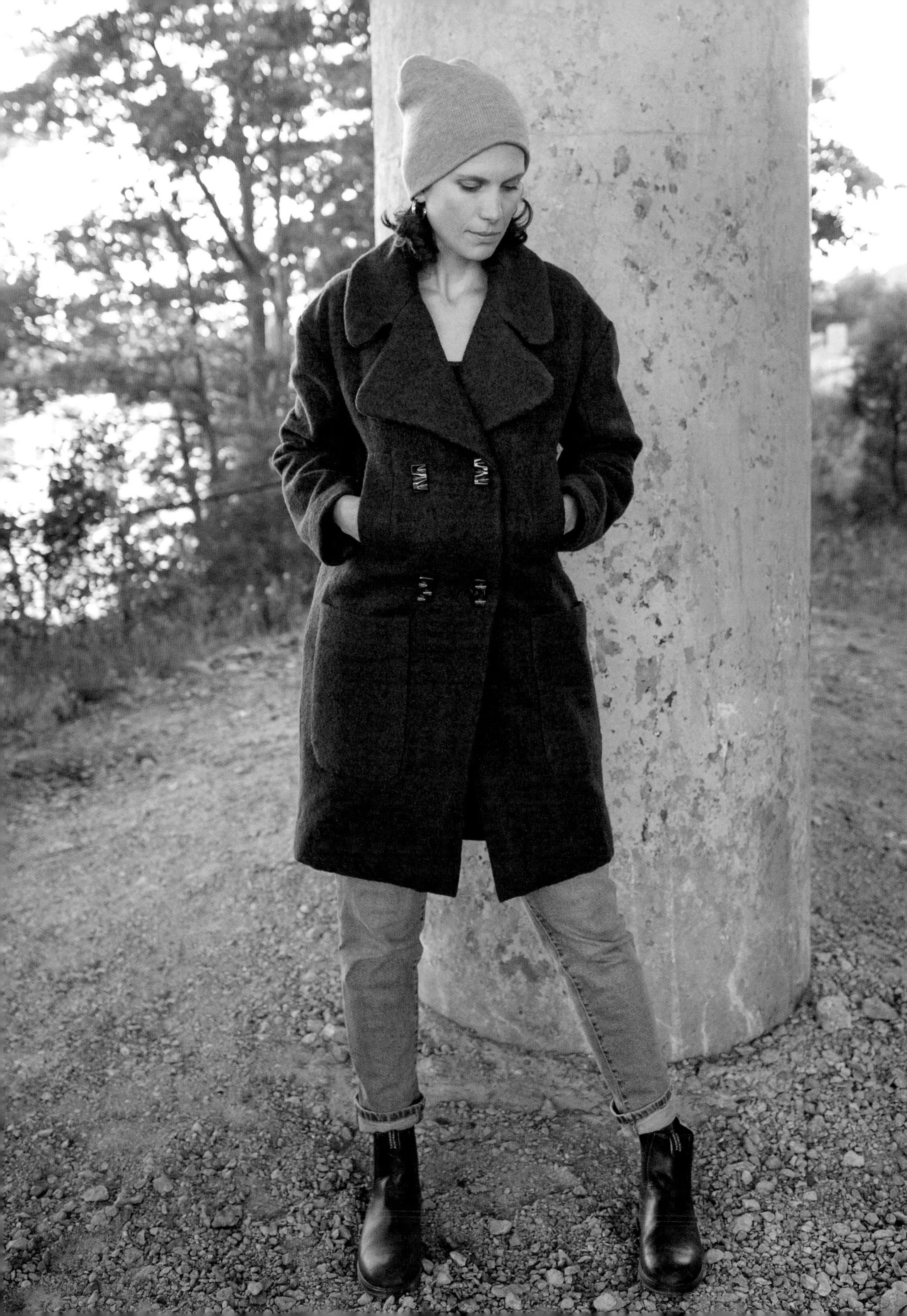

INSEAM POCKETS

Inseam pockets appear in so many patterns. These pockets, made with the familiar teardrop pattern pieces, should disappear into the seam. I feel this is a lot to ask from several extra layers of fabric. That said, it is possible to make highly functional inseam pockets that stay put and blend in smoothly.

LOOK FAMILIAR?

This _F.A.I.L._ illustrates the tendency of so many inseam pockets to look slightly lumpy along the side seams and to float or twist around inside the garment.

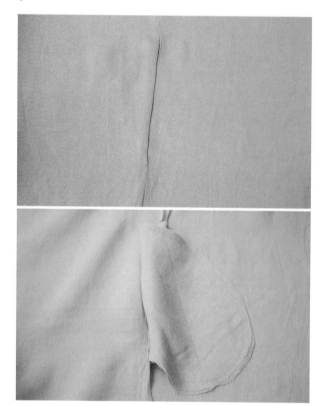

WHY THIS HAPPENS

Many of the difficulties with inseam pockets can be traced to too much bulk, either provided by the pocket bag itself under the garment front, or by congestion in the small areas where the pocket meets the side seams. Additionally, the pivot points out to the pocket in the seam allowance are stitched over four layers of fabric. This secures a lump that is pretty hard to ignore or press flat, even with clipping right to the pivot.

This pocket also demonstrates the hazards of trying to pull cut edges together, even when they don't quite match. In this case, when you stitch the pocket pieces to the side seams and press them toward the front of the garment, the pocket bag sewn to the back of the garment, lies flat and the one in front is folded—an action that will shrink it in size slightly. Ignoring this reality and trying to stitch them together matching the cut edges, is likely to produce an inseam pocket that never quite lies smoothly.

The main issue with inseam pockets is more one of design and not construction. With no other attachment to the garment than at the side seams, these little teardrop-shape units have no reason not to spin around.

FIX IT RIGHT NOW

The first and quickest fix is to unpick the pocket, throw it away, close the seam and decide you don't really need pockets. This tactic will not give you a place to put your phone and your keys.

Alternately, you can unpick the stitching along the outer edge of the pocket bags, press and trim the two layers so they are the same size, accounting for turn of cloth in the front piece, and then restitch them together. Stitching the pocket bags to the garment fronts and backs with a smaller seam allowance than the side seams will also help to hide the pocket opening. Understitching (page 164) the front pocket bag to its seam allowance will also help keep the entire pocket facing forward.

If all these tactics doesn't give you the pocket you want, simply remove the old units and install new ones with the methods that follow.

Extra Prep for Pocket Success

Following these two extra steps as you prepare your pockets will help you achieve sturdier pockets that stay in place.

FACE THE POCKET

I find it is usually necessary to face the edges of all inseam pockets in heavier fabric. Just cut the pocket bags out of a lighter fabric and apply a 1½″ (4cm) strip of garment fabric along the side seam edge of each pocket bag and continue with constructing the garment as usual. Once stitched to the side seams of the garment piece, make sure to understitch (page 164) the front pocket piece to its seam allowance.

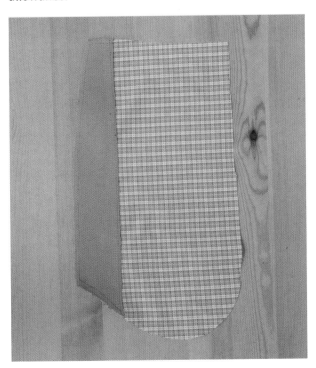

REINFORCE THE CLIPPING AREA

One of the secrets for getting the pocket bag to stay in place, facing the front, is to reinforce the area where the clip liberates the back pocket bag so it can lie toward the front. I find that this is often not necessary when working with lighter fabrics but is required when working with bulkier fabrics. Clip at the pocket attachment marks on the back pattern pieces only.

When I prepare the garment pieces, before I start to sew and clip, I usually iron a small piece of fusible interfacing (a fusible knit tricot because it adds stability but not bulk) to the small area where the side seam and the pocket seams will meet. This reinforcement will make you braver when it is time to clip the intersection of these seams.

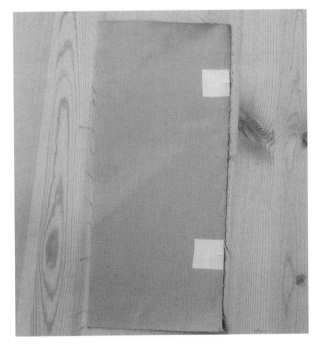

Construct the Pocket in Two Steps

Many patterns say to sew the side seam, pivot out and sew around the pocket bag, pivot back and complete the side seam—all in one continuous line of stitching. This was the method used to construct the _F.A.I.L._ pocket.

I find it more useful to break up the process. I stop to clip and trim, and avoid any stitching over more than two layers at a time. This is a simple idea, but it makes a huge difference to reducing congestion at the points where the pocket intersects with the side seams.

1. Stitch a pocket bag to the front and to the back pieces with a smaller seam allowance than standard seam allowance.

2. Sew the full side seams above and below the pocket, stopping the stitching at the mark (this may be a dot on the pattern piece) for the pocket opening. Press seams open.

3. Flip the front of the garment out of the way to expose the pocket pieces. Smooth these so they lie flat, but don't expect the cut edges to match. If necessary, trim so they match and lie flat when pinned together.

4. Folding the side seam allowances out of the way so they won't be caught in the stitching, stitch the pocket bag together, beginning and ending at the side-seam stitches. Not crossing the seam allowances is the secret of avoiding that permanently stitched-in lump.

Reengineer the Pocket Bag

Another easy way to avoid in-seam pocket angst might be to find alternatives to the provided pocket pattern piece. There are several approaches.

REPLACE THE POCKET PIECES WITH RECTANGLES

One of my personal sewing rules is that it is always easier to cut to fit than fit to the cut. Try replacing the pocket pattern pieces with fabric rectangles. Trim the rectangles into the teardrop shape after you sew them to the side seam and press them toward the front of the garment. I generally make the rectangles slightly larger than the pattern pocket pieces—about the size of a paper pattern envelope.

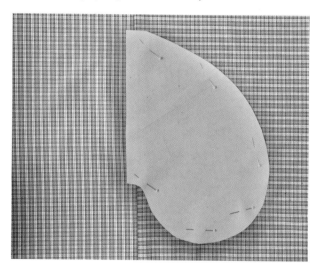

Pocket pattern piece pinned to a pocket rectangle after it has been sewn to the garment

EXTEND THE POCKET PIECE

Redraft the standard teardrop pocket piece to extend up to the waist. This works well in any garment (pants, skirts, or dress) with a waistline seam.

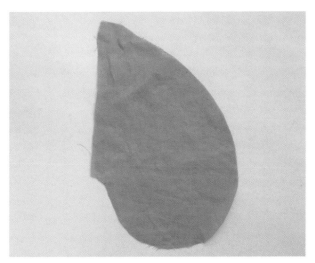

Original pocket piece

Extended pocket piece

1. Stitch a pocket bag to the front and to the back piece with a smaller seam allowance than standard seam allowance.

2. Pin the side seams together and stitch, at a full seam allowance, down from the waist to the pocket opening and again at the end of the pocket. (See the pink stitching.)

3. Move the seam allowances, side seam, and the ones that attached the pocket, away from the pocket bag so they won't catch. Stitch around the pocket. (See the green stitching line.)

4. Baste the top of both pocket layers to the front of the garment. This makes a secure pocket that won't move in the garment.

Consider a One-Layer Pocket

An extended pocket piece also can be used to make a stable one-layer faux slant pocket. This method involves visible topstitching on the right side of the garment. However, it produces the flattest inseam pocket treatment. Because of the topstitching, I feel this works best in patterned fabric or for casual styles.

1. Working first with the back garment pieces before any side seams are sewn, cut only one pocket piece for each side. This can be done as either as a rectangle sewn right sides together to the garment back, or as an extended pocket piece cut as one with the garment back.

2. Working with the front garment pieces, cut a slant along the front piece and reinforce this slant with a strip of fusible interfacing or with stay tape. When I use this method, I usually make the seam allowance a bit wider in this area at the cutting stage.

3. Turn under, press, and topstitch the edge.

4. Lay the back pocket piece behind the front, matching the edges of the waistline. Baste the top of the pocket piece to the front waistline edge.

5. Working on the right side, using the original pocket pattern piece or a good eye, draw a pocket shape with chalk or another removable marker on the front of the garment at the pocket opening.

6. Stitch the pocket to the front, right up to the waistline. I suggest doing this stitching from the right side for accuracy and to avoid unexpected puckers. (Instead of matching thread I used the bright green so you can see the stitching here.) Baste the side of the pocket to the side seams.

7. Stitch the side seam through all layers, pocket included, treating the front/pocket unit as one piece.

8. Press.

WELT, BOUND, AND FLAP POCKETS

There are many versions of pockets in the welt family, but they are all based in the same principle, a hidden pocket accessible only through a slot cut right through the main fabric of the garment.

This slot is usually filled with a flap, double-fabric lips or welts (much like a bound buttonhole) or with a single welt. A single welt may fill the slot, like the back welt pocket on men's pants, or extend and be topstitched to either side of the opening like in a coat pocket.

The multiple steps and many pattern pieces in most patterns can make these pockets seem very intimidating. However, if you are willing to deconstruct the assembly of these pockets to their essentials, I really feel any of these pockets can be very easy, and fun, to make.

The trick is to separate the slot-facing job from the pocket-making job and the welt- or flap-inserting job. I have found that treating the process as three distinct steps (most patterns suggest sewing multiple layers together as one step) with pauses between each for fine-tuning, makes all the difference. Once the opening is faced, the formula for adding welts and securing a pocket behind the opening is the same no matter what style of pocket you want. Understand how to make one of these pockets, and you can make them all.

Let's start with the most basic interpretation of the formula: the double-welt or -bound pocket.

Double-Welt Pockets

LOOK FAMILIAR?

And you tried so hard. Despite that, this carefully made pocket is probably a _F.A.I.L._ It's nice and straight, the welts look even and the same size, but those corners and ends … no other comment necessary.

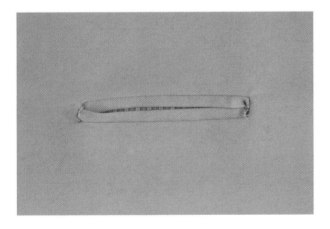

WHY THIS HAPPENS

The instructions were followed scrupulously. Unfortunately, most of the sewing activity was performed from the wrong side blind, and that sort of shows in the result. The welts or _lips_ of this pocket were made with separate strips that were basted to the slash area and then covered with the pocket opening facing. Stitching through all those layers and then trimming and turning to the right side is just too much activity in the tiny areas at the end of the pocket, particularly when you can't see what you are doing. Plus, this fabric was undoubtedly too heavy to be used in a double welt. A single welt would have been a more realistic choice.

I would give up on trying to fit this unit. I know from much bitter experience that unpicking, more clipping and even vigorous pressing are quite likely to make it worse and even frayed. Best to take a deep philosophical breath, take it all out, and try again with the multiple-step process described next.

NEXT TIME

This method simplifies the process so much by breaking it down into two distinct jobs—facing the opening and filling it with the welts.

Face the Opening

1. Press a piece of knit fusible interfacing to the pocket area on the wrong side of the garment, behind where the pocket will be stitched. The pocket is going to need this support.

2. Cut a single fabric rectangle to make the facing for each pocket opening and the welts. Make sure that this piece is at least 2″ (5cm) longer than the pocket opening and about 8 times wider than the pocket opening itself and is cut with the same grain lines as the garment front. For example, if the pocket opening is 6″ × ½″ (15 × 1cm), cut a rectangle 8″ × 4″ (20 × 10cm).

3. Pin the rectangle to the front of the garment, right sides together, centered over the intended pocket position.

Make the Welts

1. Trace a stitching box for each pocket opening onto paper, one for each pocket. Pin this over the pocket/garment right where the pocket opening will be made. I often use a lined sheet from an exercise book—the lines are already drawn for me.

2. Using a shorter-than-usual stitch length, stitch around the pocket box through the layers of paper and fabric. To avoid weakening the corners, start and stop the stitching in the middle of one long side. Tear away the paper.

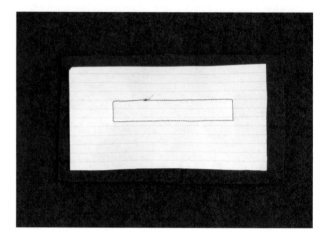

3. Slash down the middle of the stitching box and out to each corner. Trim the seam allowances to reduce bulk.

4. Pull the entire unit through to the wrong side and press to make sure there is a nice, neat faced pocket opening. If there are any puckers in the corner, go back and make sure you have clipped right to the corner. Press.

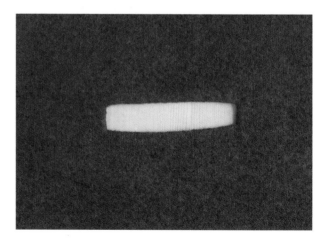

5. Return to the right side and arrange the facing fabric to fill the opening with two nice neat, even welt "lips." Press and loosely baste the welt lips together. This basting will keep them in position as you proceed with construction.

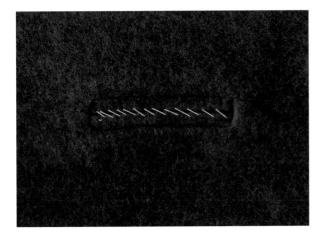

6. Secure the lips in position. There are three options for this.

• Working from the right side, make hand stitches through all layers in the well of the stitching all around the pocket opening. This is probably the easiest and fastest method. If you want more security, later you can use a zipper foot to machine stitch the edges of the welts to the seam allowances around the pocket opening as described in optional Step 7.

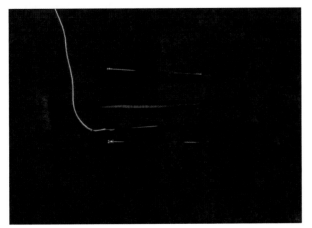

Here are the usual prick stitches (page 167) buried in the seam more or less invisibly.

• Work from the right side and machine stitch-in-the-ditch all around the pocket opening.

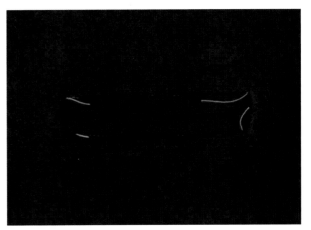

The ditch stitching here was done in green fluorescent thread. When pressed, these stitches should disappear in the well of the seam.

• Topstitch the perimeter of the opening. This is the method used most often in ready-to-wear garments. Not something I do myself, but a possibility.

7. *Optional:* Carefully, working from the wrong side of the garment, and using a zipper foot and a straight stitch, sew the long edges of the welts to the seam allowance around the pocket opening as closely as you can to the existing stitching. It is not necessary to stitch across the ends of the welts, as that will be dealt with when the pocket bags are attached.

Add the Pocket Bags

Not surprisingly, I do not cut out two pocket pieces. My own preference is to make the pocket bags out of one rectangle of cotton (a fine twill is ideal because it is strong) that is folded to make the pocket. One end of this pocket rectangle can be faced with a strip of garment fabric behind the opening if the pocket fabric is very different than the garment fabric. If the fabric is bulky, apply the facing piece below the seam allowance, turning under and topstitching the raw edges.

This pocket piece should be as wide as the pocket opening plus 2″ (5cm) and twice the depth of the pocket plus ½″ (1cm), which allows for two ¼″ (0.5cm) seam allowances.

1. Fold the pocket bag in half and stitch each short end to the pocket opening / welt seam allowances.

2. Press the pocket bag down and allow the pocket to fall naturally into shape. Stitch both sides of the pocket, catching in the ends of the welts, to finish these seam allowances. If you haven't already serge-finished the pocket fabric, you can zigzag these seam allowances now.

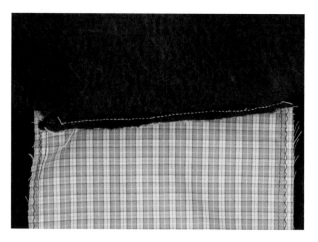

3. Press from the wrong side and, with a pressing cloth, again from the right side.

Basic Single-Welt Pockets

These single-welt pockets are used primarily as back pockets in tailored pants, for breast pockets in jackets, or as interior pockets in linings, especially in menswear. In linings and at the back of pants, they may have a button loop and button at the top for added security.

The process for making a simple single welt is a variation of the method for a double welt. The only difference is that rather than arranging two lips as in Make the Welts, Step 5 (page 77), just arrange one large welt to fill the slot space. Then follow the rest of the construction steps.

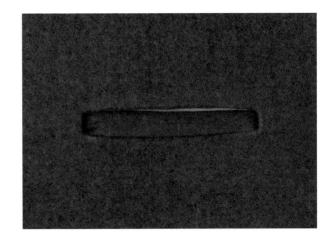

When making a heavy-use pocket, like in the back of a pair of pants, topstitch around the opening for strength.

Separate Single-Welt Pockets

Separate single-welt pockets are the most common, and practical, form of welt pockets for heavy coats and jackets. In this application, a large welt is sewn into the pocket opening and the ends of the welt are top-stitched to either side for strength and durability.

LOOK FAMILIAR?

This *F.A.I.L.* almost made it. The welt sits neatly on the front of the coat but when stitched and pulled to the right side, as per the pattern, it has hauled some of the garment with it, making folds at each end of the welt. Also, and this would be the upsetting part, the welt doesn't quite cover the slot and some of the pocket fabric is peeking through.

This has happened to all of us. The pocket bags were cut out to match exactly, but due to the influence of turn of cloth, one pocket appears to have shrunk and one has grown. As a consequence, trying to make the cut edges match produced a pleat in the stitching.

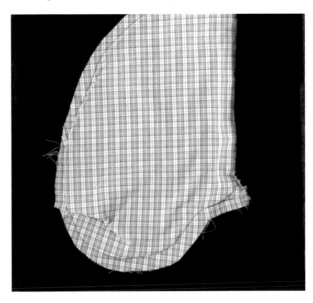

WHY THIS HAPPENS

This _**F.A.I.L.**_ was constructed exactly as instructed in the pattern using exactly the pattern pieces supplied. Neither the pattern nor the instructions considered the reality of turn of cloth. Wrapping all those layers through the cut opening and pulling them through makes the welt itself smaller and then covering all edges of the welt opening very difficult. Also, neglecting turn of cloth left the pocket bag pieces hard to make lie flat.

FIX IT RIGHT NOW

Well, you could cry. Or you can unpick the whole thing, have a cup of tea, and try again using the method below. If you just can't face starting over, you can appliqué a slightly longer rectangle of a nonwoven fabric such as leather or faux suede carefully over the welt, extending it to cover any messy parts at the end of the welt. I have sometimes done that by stitching the suede to the top of the welt and then topstitching the remaining three sides to the garment. Desperate times call for desperate measures.

NEXT TIME

The traditional methods of inserting single-welt pockets often assume that dimensional fabric will behave the same way as paper or a two-dimensional drawing. Rather than the multiple pattern pieces suggested in the pattern, my approach uses a large piece of fabric that can be trimmed to fit after the pocket has been turned to the inside. It also uses a welt piece preshaped to cover any potential issues.

Adjust the Welt and Pocket Patterns

Your pattern may suggest the welt be made of two pieces stitched together and two shaped pieces for the pocket bag. This is what I do instead.

1. Use a fold for the top of the welt piece, rather than two pieces of fabric that need to be seamed. This will reduce bulk.

2. When stitching the welt sides together, angle the stitching lines out ⅛″ (3mm) toward the fold/top. This will give the welt a slight flange that will reach over and cover the pocket slot easily. This is so, so important and makes such a difference.

3. Ditch those pattern pieces and use one big piece of fabric for the pocket bag.

The pocket/facing piece should be about 3″ (8cm) wider than the welt opening and twice as long as the intended pocket bag plus another 3″ (8cm) in length, and cut on the same grain as the garment front.

Sew the Pocket

1. Make the welt. Grade the seams (see Grade, page 163), and turn and press. Baste the raw edges together. Topstitch around the finished edges.

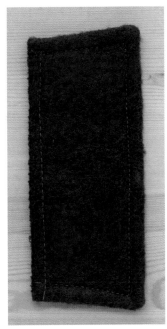

2. Pin the welt next to the welt markings on the garment front. The cut and basted-together edges of the welt should meet the marked cutting line at the center of any welt placement markings.

3. Stitch the welt in place ¼″ (0.5cm) from this centerline:

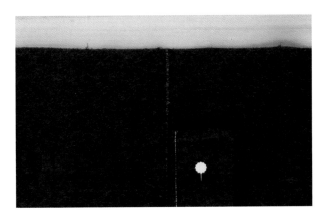

4. Fold the pocket/facing in half in the middle and press.

5. On the right side of the garment, unfold the pocket/facing and lay it over the welt with the pressed line positioned over the cut edge of the welt, which has been stitched to the centerline. You might have to do this a bit by feel. Pin all around the edges of the pocket/facing piece to attach it securely to the garment front.

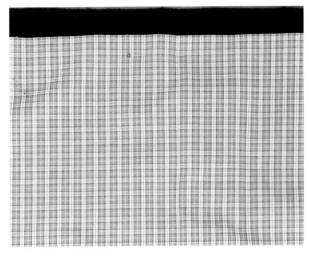

6. Working from the wrong side, stitch another row of stitching directly over the stitching line that attached the welt, securing the pocket lining to one side of what will be the pocket opening. (See the pink thread in the photo under Step 7, page 82.)

7. Stitch another row of stitching, parallel to and ½″ (1cm) from the stitching line in Step 6, making the second side of the pocket opening. (See the bright green thread.)

However—*and this is really, really important*—make this second line of stitching about ¼″ (0.5cm) shorter on both ends than the first stitching line. This little maneuver will ensure that the pocket slot angles in slightly at the top which, combined with the slight angle-out shape of the top of the welt, will eliminate any problem with having the ends of the welt cover the opening.

8. Cut the welt slot open, down the middle and out to the end of each line of stitching, making sizable V's that are easy to hold onto. Try not to cut into the welt. I find this step easier if I cut through each layer, the garment fabric and the pocketing, one at a time.

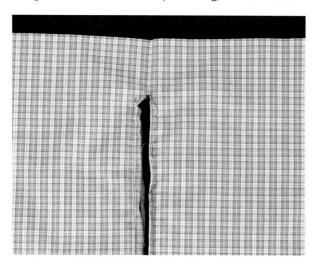

9. Pull the pocket/facing to the inside and press, pulling the welt up. Arrange and then press the pocketing/facing away from the slot opening. You can see here, on the wrong side how the opening slants in, creating a hiding space for the opening behind the welt.

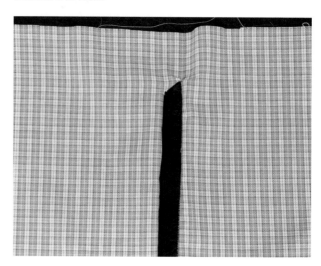

10. On the wrong side of the garment, let the upper part of the pocket/facing fall naturally, forming the pocket bag.

11. Fold the pocket bag back on each side, exposing the little wedge where the opening was cut. Stitch across this wedge at the sides with a few low-stress rows of machine stitching and try to curve this in slightly to counteract the pull of turn of cloth.

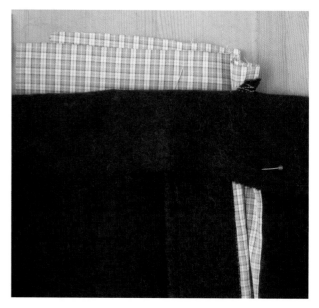

12. Stitch the sides of the pocket bag closed below the welt, then stitch again or add a zigzag for reinforcement.

13. Secure the ends of the welt to the garment. Often this is done from the right side with machine stitching if those sides of the welt have not already been topstitched. However, since stitching through so many layers can be difficult, I usually do this with a hand backstitch (page 164), working from the wrong side. More relaxing.

Flap Pockets

The faced slot used as a base for the double- and single-welt pocket can be a foundation for other styles of pocket. One of my favorites is a welt pocket with a flap—a style of pocket particularly suited to outerwear as the flap protects the interior of pocket from snow, rain, and sleet.

There are many methods for adding a flap to a double, or even single welt. Frankly, I find most of them horrifying. Those other methods involve making a flap and basting it to the markings for the pocket opening, actually underneath the welt lips, before that opening is made. The idea is that once all these many layers are stitched through and the whole thing slashed open, it will all turn to the right side and look great. In my opinion, even Harry Houdini would have a hard time getting this process to work. Usually the flaps end up being too big or too small for the opening and the bulk in the pocket seams keeps the whole enterprise from lying flat.

It's much simpler to just make up a nice flap, slide it into the finished pocket opening to confirm it fits, and then baste it into position. Stitching the pocket bag in will secure it. Why make life harder than that?

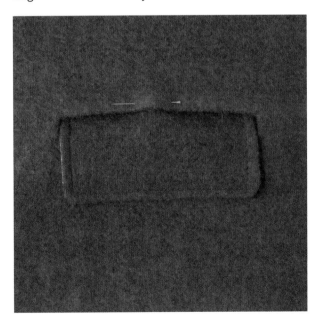

Zippered Pockets

Adding a zipper behind the slot opening is too easy. A large rectangle of pocketing fabric is used to face the opening, the zipper is stitched in, and the fabric allowed to fall and form the pocket.

1. Pin a large rectangle of fabric to the front of the garment, right sides together. Pin paper with the stitching box over these layers.

2. Stitch over the marked box with a small stitch length, starting and stopping in the middle of one long side.

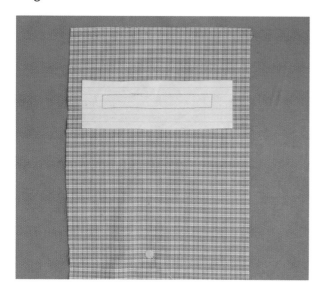

3. Slash through the middle of the opening and out to the corners.

4. Pull the pocket/facing fabric to the wrong side. Adjust to make a clean opening and press.

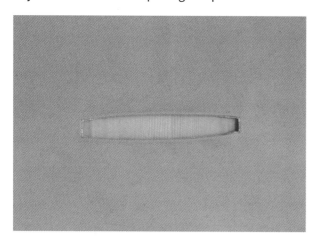

5. Lay the zipper behind the opening and topstitch it in place around all edges.

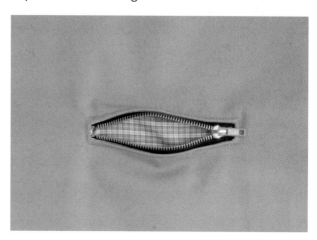

6. On the wrong side, let the pocket/facing fabric fall naturally behind the opening. Mark a pocket shape and stitch. Catch the small triangles at the ends of the opening in this stitching. Trim and finish the raw edges.

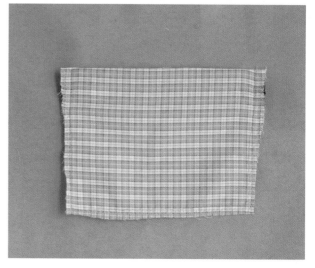

Double-Patch Pockets

Many patterns for jackets and coats in lofty or textured fabrics call for patch pockets. In principle, these should be the easiest outwear pocket to make, but in practice the results can look unprofessional.

In this *F.A.I.L.*, every attempt was made to topstitch the patch pocket as suggested by the pattern. Unfortunately, it's difficult to do evenly over the layers and, to my mind, the machine stitches clash with the loft of the fabric.

WHY THIS HAPPENS

The issue is treating every detail as if it should be done the exact same way despite differences in fabric. This way of applying a pocket would be just fine in a linen or other flat fabric, but a soft fabric suits a softer construction method.

FIX IT RIGHT NOW

This pocket needs to be removed and stitched again. To topstitch more effectively, in keeping with the proportion and hand of the fabric, use a much longer stitch length and a heavier thread, and don't try to stitch close to the edge. A rule of thumb is to topstitch a distance from the edge that is similar to two layers of the fabric. In this case, that would be almost a presser-foot distance from the edge.

NEXT TIME

Coat pockets in fabric like this require some strategic thinking. First, the pocket itself needs a gentle application that situates the pocket but blends it into the surface of the thick, soft fabric. A pocket secured "invisibly" with hand stitches will do this. Second, this pocket has to be strong and sturdy, a completely different objective altogether. The solution to these conflicting specifications is to layer two pockets: one on the outside for appearance and one underneath it for utility.

This double-patch pocket is one of my favorites—always elegant, always durable.

1. Cut out the patch pocket and fuse a strip of interfacing to the back of the top edges. This reinforcement will help to keep the pocket from bagging.

2. Press under the seam allowances around all but the top hem edge.

3. Mark the pocket placement on the garment front. I like thread tracing for accuracy. *Thread tracing* is just a line of basting stitches. A simple way to do this is to use a tracing wheel and dressmakers carbon paper placed under the pattern to transfer the pocket outline to the wrong side of the fabric. Baste over these markings, working from the wrong side, so this important information can be seen from the right side of the fabric.

4. For a pocket lining, cut a rectangle of close-weave pocketing fabric a little bigger than the pocket. I always use cotton, never lining fabric. For hand-friendly cold-weather pockets, try cotton flannel. Stitch this fabric to the top of the pocket markings, right sides together. Press.

5. Right sides together, pin the lining side of the pocket unit over the pocket area of the garment. Make sure the pocketing is laid an upper hem allowance distance below the top of pocket marking.

6. Smooth the pocket piece down over the lining, folding it at the hem line at the top of the pocket, and trace this shape onto the lining as a template.

7. Move the pocket piece back up and stitch the pocket shape through all layers, aiming to keep the stitches just inside the pocket marking. Use a small, close zigzag to finish and secure the pocket in one step.

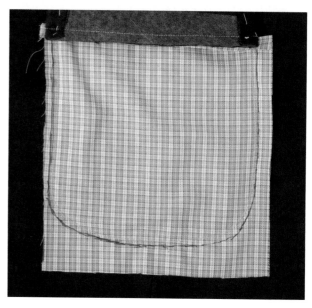

8. Trim away the extra fabric from around the pocket.

9. Fold the garment pocket down over the inner pocket. Pin in place, making sure that all the edges of the pocket underneath are covered.

10. Working from the outside, hand stitch the pocket to the garment with a discreet slip stitch (page 168).

11. To reinforce the pocket even further, turn to the wrong side and sew a second row of hand stitches, using a backstitch (page 164) or prick stitch (page 167). Aim to catch the pocket's pressed seam allowances in these stitches, but make sure none show through on the right side.

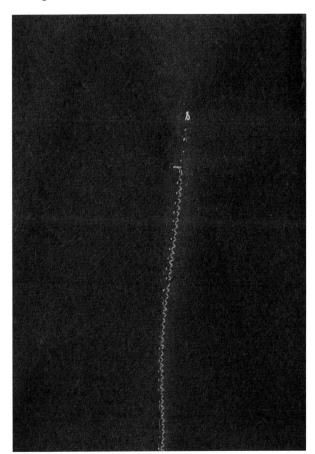

BONUS POCKET: THE INSTA CELL-PHONE POCKET

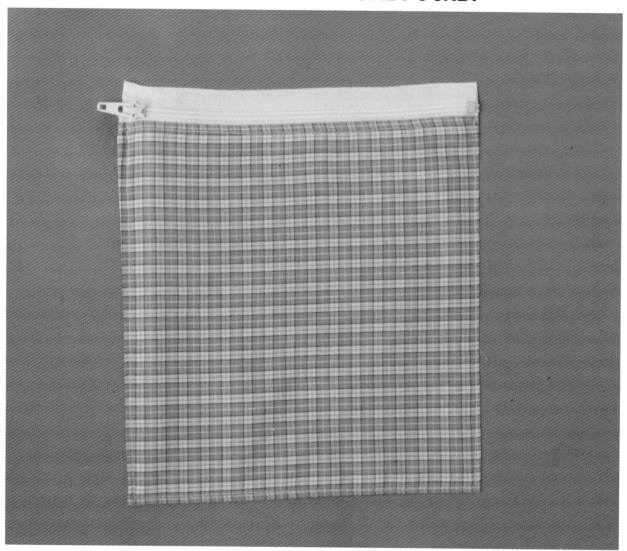

I can't resist sharing this. Interior pockets are very useful. They are good for a lot of things, but most of all, your cell phone. Very often these inside pockets are designed to be made with a double-welt opening and often with a button and fabric loop to keep the contents secure. You can make your hidden pockets this way too, and I'd say good for you.

However, if you share my utility view of this kind of pocket, you might be interested in the fast but effective zippered pocket I often make myself. This very simple zippered patch pocket can be added to anything where a safe inside pocket would be useful. I put them in most of my outerwear, all of my bags, and inside anything that any school-age child might wear. We lost very many notes from the teacher until I instituted these pockets in all the kids' jackets.

These pockets can be added to any lining before it is inserted in the garment. Based on the size of your phone or other items, the pocket bag can be any size you want. The only bit of preplanning: Remember which is your wearer's dominant hand and therefore which side of the lining the pocket should be sewn into. A lefty's pocket should be on the right lining, and a right-handed person's on the left. Also make sure the zipper pull at the top of the pocket is to the back of the garment once worn. Being able to unzip the pocket by pulling the tab toward the front is always so much easier.

You need a rectangle of pocketing fabric and a dress-weight zipper, preferably a bit longer than the finished width of the pocket.

1. Press under the seam allowances on the bottom and side edges of the pocket piece. Do not turn under the top seam allowance.

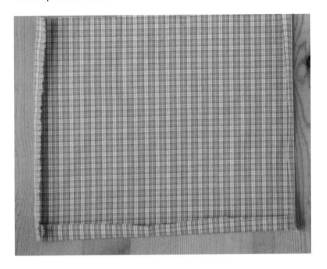

2. Unfold the pressed seam allowances. Lay the zipper facedown on the right side of the pocket, the edge of the zipper tape even with the raw edge of the top of the pocket. Using a zipper foot, stitch the zipper to the pocket. Turn the zipper up.

3. From the right side, topstitch along the zipper tape close to the teeth.

4. Pin the pocket piece to the garment lining. Tuck under the ends of the zipper, turn under the seam allowances around the pocket, pin and stitch around the three sides of the pocket.

5. Pin and then topstitch the upper zipper tape directly to the garment lining.

Done.

Chapter 6

Zippers

If you sew garments in woven fabric, you sew zippers. Not many ways around it—not that many of us don't try. But there are only so many garments you want to close with a button or snaps. Not many little black dresses fasten at the back with hook-and-loop tape.

A sewist just has to get zipper-friendly. Unfortunately, most patterns don't provide enough how-to. Is it always necessary to finish the top of a zipper at the back neck with a hook and eye? What do you do about that gap between the top of a zipper and a waistband? Is it possible to sew in a lapped zipper right the first time? Are invisible zippers only for advanced sewists? Of the 49 methods for putting in a fly front, which is the easiest? And is it possible to put a zipper in a fine fabric, such as silk, velvet, or crepe, without losing your mind?

I think I have figured out my own answers to each of these questions. It's my life mission. My aim is to put together a toolbox of simple but effective construction techniques so I can enjoy my sewing without worrying about it at all.

This process has taken me some time. For every method I have decided works well for me, I had to experiment with many that didn't. I want to save you that trouble. I want to get you to feeling zipper-relaxed as fast as I can. That's what this chapter is about.

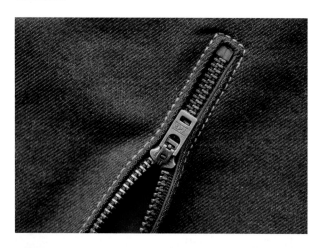

BACK ZIPPERS

I once met a very nice woman in parking lot who showed me the dresses she had sewn. They were all lovely with centered back zippers, but she was fairly distraught over how they all looked—wonky stitching and a space at the top. I felt for her. Here is a replication of her *F.A.I.L.*s.

Centered Back Zipper

LOOK FAMILIAR?

The topstitching lines are not equal distance from the seamline in this *F.A.I.L.*, the zipper ends too far from the stitching line that will attach the facings, and the stitching bumps around the zipper pull.

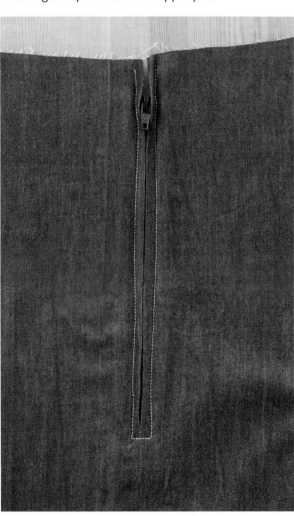

WHY THIS HAPPENS

The issue of the uneven stitching lines is hard to rectify without a do-over. At this point you can either write this one off as an educational experience (an option I have often used) or unpick the whole thing and try one of the alternate methods below.

NEXT TIME

Centered zippers are possible with attention to even spacing between the two lines of topstitching. A strip of clear adhesive tape carefully centered over the seamline makes a great stitching guide. This is a useful tactic when a centered zipper is called for in a front zippered jacket, for example. However, I don't see the need for centered zippers in the back of garments. To my mind, this is a somewhat dated technique and why worry about keeping two lines of topstitching straight when you can only worry about one, or even none?

Instead, I usually install invisible zippers in my dresses, tops, and many of my skirts and pants. I also use a streamlined method for lap zippers for the occasional dress and often for side and back zippers in pants and skirts. Both are so easy to do.

Invisible Back Zipper

Invisible zippers are so easy, but this one has definite _F.A.I.L._ characteristics and looks like most first attempts. Portions of the zipper tape show, making this zipper anything but invisible. And there is a little bump in the fabric, made when attempting to meet the end of the zipper, stitching exactly with the seam below the zipper and stitching this seam up toward the zipper and not down from it.

The problem is either not using a designated zipper foot, not trusting that foot, or not appreciating the wonderful option this application has to stitch and restitch along the zipper until you get it right. The usual instruction to sew the seam up to meet the end of the stitching on the zipper is hard to get right. So often the zipper stop gets in the way, and that's not your fault.

Correctly Inserting an Invisible Zipper

Inserting an invisible zipper is easiest technique you'll find in this book. Invisible zippers are sewn onto the right side of the fabric and installed with coils rolled open so they lie exactly over the seamline. This may seem complicated, but with a special foot that does all the work, it's a piece of cake.

1. You are going to need a special foot, one designed for your own brand of machine. Yes, I know the generic versions sold in fabric stores say they fit every machine, and they kinda do, but the parts are wobbly. And I know there are folks who just use a narrow or zipper foot to install invisible zippers and good for them. I even used to try this myself until I sewed right through a finger trying to spread the zipper coils. Using a designated foot is just so much easier. The grooves on the bottom of a built-for-your-machine invisible zipper foot hold the coils very securely and guide the stitching right next to the coils. Having this much taken care of by the foot allows your hands, and maybe your mind, to be totally irresponsible for the whole process. That's relaxed sewing to me.

Tip **Finding the Groove**

If you find using an invisible zipper foot confusing, repeat after me, "Left side of the garment, left groove; for the right side, right groove." And of course, always install the zipper right side down on the right side of the fabric and with the zipper tape always facing the finished edge of the seam allowance, _not_ into the garment.

2. Press under the seam allowances along the seamline. Having this press line as a point of reference is very useful, because much of the technique requires accurate placement of the teeth along the seamline.

3. Put both halves of the garment into which the zipper will be inserted together on a table, right sides facing you. Start with the left side first and lay the zipper facedown on the right side of the garment fabric, with the zipper tape closest to the edge of the opening, and the coils lined up exactly over the seam stitching line.

Make sure the top coil is a seam-allowance distance below the top edge of the garment. Note where the zipper ends on the bottom seamline and place a mark 1″ (2.5cm) above this. That's where the garment seam will be stitched later on. You will sew each side of the zipper from the top to bottom to help keep the sides even.

4. Sew the left side of the zipper. *Remember:* Left side, use left groove. Lift the presser foot and make sure that the left groove in the foot is fitted over the zipper coil. The trick of using the foot is to get this initial fit snug, but after that to let the foot do the work. Don't try to uncoil the zipper yourself more than is necessary to guide the stitching. Stitch to as far as you can toward the zipper stop, but don't expect to get all the way there. Remove the work and close the zipper. If any tape shows at the seamline, just restitch it until you are satisfied. I usually need two tries to get it perfect.

5. Sew the right side of the zipper. Again, lay the zipper facedown on the right side of the garment fabric, with the zipper tape closest to the edge of the opening, and the coils lined up exactly over the seam stitching line. *Remember:* Right side, use right groove. Close the zipper to confirm the two sides are even, then open the zipper and lay the right side of the zipper over the right side of the garment, with the coil in the groove in the right side of the foot. Take some time to check that the zipper isn't flipped or

twisted. Sew this side of the zipper from the top to as far down as you can go. Note this will mean that the body of the garment is to the right of the needle.

Here is how the zipper looks from the right side installed.

6. Replace the invisible zipper foot with a conventional foot. This will give the stability needed to stitch the bulk of the structural seam. However, feel free to start with an ordinary zipper foot for the first little bit of the seam if you find it easier.

7. Pin the seam below the zipper, starting at the mark made 1″ (2.5cm) above the zipper stop. Move the free zipper tape to the side and out of the way while you pin.

8. Sew the seam down past the bottom of the zipper. Stitch down from the zipper, not up. This stitching direction will eliminate any little bubbles of grain direction backing up under the end of the zipper. When you start to sew this seam, don't try to sew exactly over the previous stitching lines but begin slightly away from them a bit into the body of the garment. This little gap in stitching is actually a good thing as it gives the coil room to settle in behind the seam.

This is how the seam blends into the zipper. The point where they meet is marked with a pin. That little gap in the stitching doesn't show at all.

9. Sew the free ends of each zipper tape to the seam allowance, by hand or by machine.

Tip Smooth Neckline Option

This is my favorite technique for tops or dresses with neck openings big enough to go over your head—install the zipper at least 2″ (5cm) below the neckline and then sew the seam above it closed, with the same method used to close the seam below the zipper. Here is how this looks. I love it!

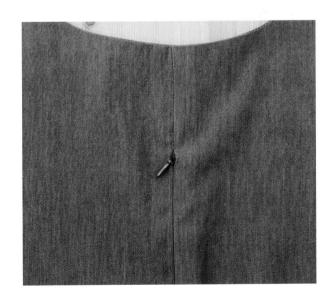

Lapped Back Zipper

There is a lot of disappointment in this **_F.A.I.L._** The stitching on the underlap shows. Attempts to haul the overlap over this to cover it up has made a pucker, and there is some crooked stitching at the bottom of the zipper. All the seam allowances on the overlap didn't quite make it into the topstitching either. And of course, trying to stitch around the zipper pull has made a bump in the topstitching.

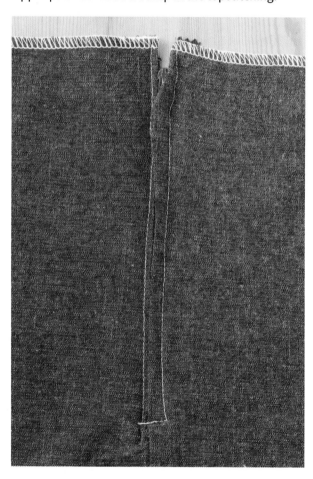

WHY THIS HAPPENS

All these issues result from trying to do so much with a normal-width seam allowance. The issue of trying to sew around the zipper pull is often inevitable when using a zipper no longer than the one specified.

FIX IT RIGHT NOW

If it was me at this stage, and to save my nerves, I would take out the topstitching and use a prick stitch (page 167) and the technique described in the hand-inserted zipper (see Alternative to a Machine-Stitched Zipper, page 105) to secure the overlap. Another alternative, though not as easy, is to take this out and get a slightly longer zipper and try again.

NEXT TIME

Buy a slightly longer zipper, so the pull can be pulled past the top of the edge for topstitching. See a similar approach in the method for inserting a zipper into a waistband (see Preventing a Waistband Gap, page 99). With a longer zipper, you also can keep the metal zipper stop at the end of the zipper out of the way.

Another small change—adding extra width to the seam allowances in the seam where the zipper will be inserted—will make a huge difference. I usually change the seam allowance widths of seams with lap zippers to 1″ (2.5cm). Having a wider seam allowance behind the lap will make topstitching much less stressful.

1. Sew the seam up to the bottom of the zipper opening.

2. Press under the lap side above the opening, making the fold exactly continuous with the seamline.

3. Press the seam allowance on the underlap side about ⅛″ (3mm) less, so that it extends slightly under the seam. There will be no need to clip, just fade the seam allowance back to full width under the opening.

4. Lay the zipper faceup with the teeth right next to the folded seam of the underlap. I usually find it easier to control this with my hands rather than with pins. Using a zipper foot, stitch close to the teeth through all layers at the edge of the fold.

Stitching the first side of the zipper to the underlapped folded edge situates that side of the zipper cleanly under the top overlap.

5. Close the seam by bringing the top edge over so the coils of the zipper are completely hidden. Quickly and casually slip baste (page 168) along the seamline to hold this fold in place over the underlap zipper teeth.

6. Again, using just your hands (I find pins can distort the fabric), smooth the zipper under the lap. Using a zipper foot, topstitch across the bottom of the opening, pivot, and stitch up the lap, feeling with your fingers for the coil of the zipper as you go.

If the zipper isn't longer than needed, when you reach the zipper pull, stop with the needle down, open the zipper, and wiggle it down past the needle. Continue stitching. Stitching up from the bottom of the zipper, rather than down, will prevent a bubble at the bottom of the opening.

If you have used a longer zipper, you can stitch right across the coils without having to worry about avoiding the zipper stop. You can trim off the excess zipper length later during construction.

7. Remove the basting and press.

PREVENTING A WAISTBAND GAP

Waistbands with a tiny gap at the top of the zipper were the bane of my high school sewing days. No matter how carefully I tried to sew the waistband as close to the zipper stops as I could, I never quite got rid of that little blouse-fabric-revealing hole. Then one day someone taught me to buy my zippers longer than the opening, and my whole world changed.

This _F.A.I.L._ was made exactly to the pattern directions. Even still, using the recommended zipper length and starting the zipper where marked, there is a gap at the top between the waistband and the top of the zipper, partially due to the metal zipper top. The next step for this waistband was to close it with a hook and eye.

Metal zipper stops prevent the top of a zipper from getting in close to the sewn-on waistband. No way around it.

The most practical immediate fix is to open up the waistband, unpick the stitches until at least the back darts, and trim off a bit of seam allowance. Resew the waistband, lowering it so the stitching line goes right over the coils beneath the zipper stop.

Buy a zipper longer than you need. The method that follows is a variation on the way zippers are sewn into fly fronts.

1. Insert the zipper as usual but leave the excess zipper/tape extending above the seamline.

I intentionally extended the waistband on this underlap side. The extension allows me to add a buttonhole (hidden from the right side) to lay under the waistband with an added button on the other side.

2. Sew on the waistband, stitching it right across the teeth of the zipper. Only then cut off the zipper tape.

3. Fold up the waistband and continue with construction. The zipper will now pull up right under the waistband without any gap. Nice and neat.

FLY ZIPPERS

LOOK FAMILIAR?

In this _F.A.I.L._, despite best efforts and following all markings, the stitching for the zipper underlap shows at the bottom of the fly. The wonky topstitching would have benefited by a little chalk marking before stitching!

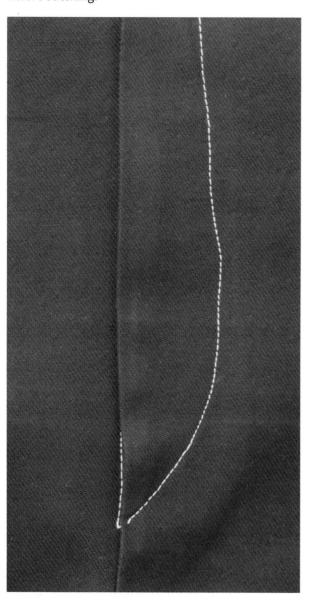

WHY THIS HAPPENS

The lesson is to let the zipper fall naturally into place behind the fly rather than trying to haul the zipper over to meet any markings.

FIX IT RIGHT NOW

The topstitching needs to be removed and redone. I would also remove and restitch the zipper tape under the overlap, using the method described below.

NEXT TIME

Once you have made a lapped zipper, you pretty much know all you need to make a great fly-front zipper. The process is nearly identical, only the scale is different. These instructions are for a women's fly; for men's pants, reverse the under/overlap stitching. Use a longer zipper than you need and sew the waistband over the top of the zipper coil as in the instructions for a Lapped Back Zipper (page 96). Note these samples show how those longer zippers look before they are captured in the waistband. Of course, if you are sewing with a metal-tooth jeans zipper, the top teeth need to end at the seamline.

1. The first thing is to simplify the pattern. No matter how many pieces you see in that envelope, if you are going to do this relaxed, all you need are fly-shaped seam extensions as part of the pattern. Your pattern may have the fly extensions as separate pieces, but I don't think the bulk of that seam is necessary. Tape the pattern pieces together if you have to, but make sure what you have looks like this, an extension of about 1¾″ (4.5cm) or more with a curve ending where the straight seam starts to bend into the crotch.

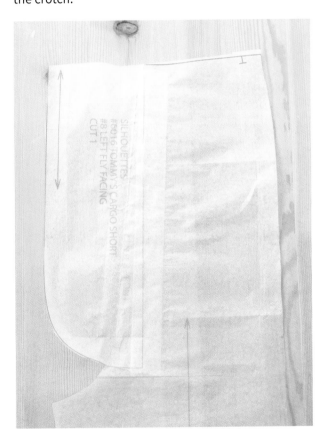

2. Interface both fly extensions to prevent ripples. I use a fusible knit interfacing cut with the stable grain of the interfacing running with the length of the extension. Finish the raw edges of the extension and the front crotch seam.

3. Sew the front crotch seam up to the waist along the extensions. Use a regular stitch length for the bottom portion of this seam, make a definite back-stitch at the dot marking the beginning of the zipper opening, and then do a machine baste right up to the waist.

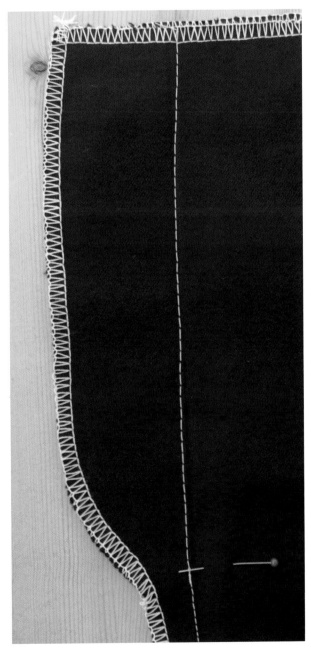

4. Press the crotch seam to one side and the extensions open, folding under one seam allowance a bit at the top of the crotch seam to do this. I prefer this to clipping to the stitch, which I feel weakens the seam at a stress point.

Turn the pants over to the wrong side and lay them on a flat surface. Move both front legs and the left extension over and out of the way. Working with only the single layer of the right extension, position the zipper *facedown*, so the zipper stop is 1″ (2.5cm) below the dot at the zipper opening, and with the left edge of the zipper tape right on the seamline.

5. Using a zipper foot, stitch along the right side of the zipper tape as closely as you can to the coil.

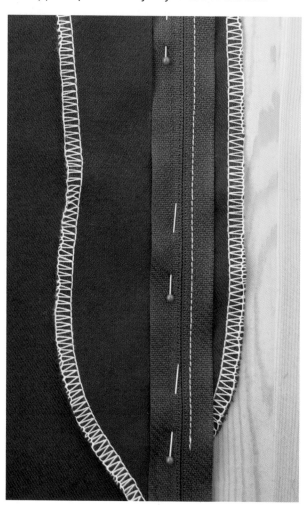

6. Flip the zipper over so the right side is facing you. Smooth and press the fly extension away from the teeth and topstitch the zipper down again, this time from the right side. First side done.

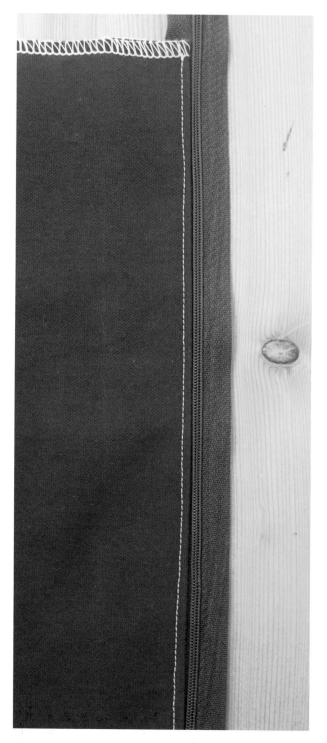

7. Open both legs and smooth the fly evenly behind the seamline. Let the remaining unstitched zipper tape fall naturally into position on the left fly. This is the secret to a fly that lies flat, don't try to force it. Pin the unstitched zipper tape to the single layer of the remaining fly extension.

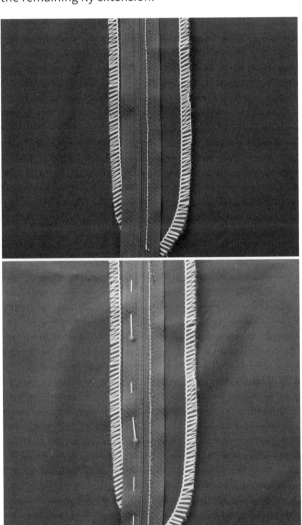

8. Again using a zipper foot, stitch the left side of the zipper tape as closely as you can to the coil. Second side done and secure, as in the pink regular stitch length line of stitching below.

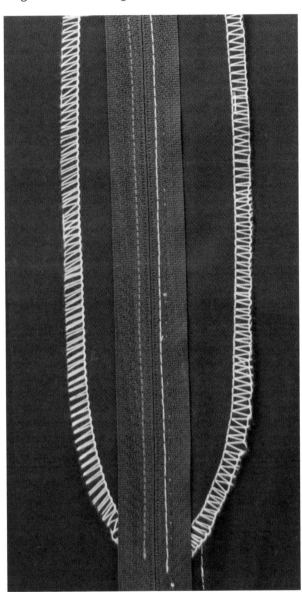

9. Turn the pants over to the right side and smooth the fly area. Now topstitch the classic fly curve, starting from the bottom and working to the top. This direction of stitching will prevent a bubble forming at the bottom of the fly. You can draw this topstitching line in. Some folks suggest a template, but I have never bothered. Relax with this topstitching. The zipper is already secure, so really the only purpose of the topstitching is to secure the fabric of the extension. Low stakes.

Remove the basting stitches and press.

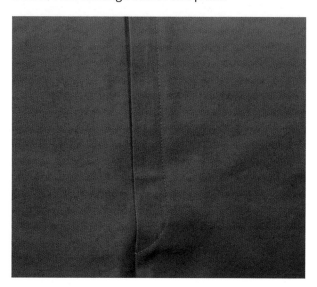

10. Make the fly guard. Sew the two layers of the guard together along the curved edges, turn, notch and press. Finish the long raw edges.

11. Open the zipper and lay the pants right side up. Arrange the guard behind the underlap side and stitch through all layers to the seam allowance.

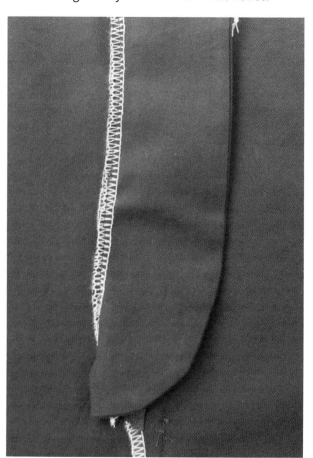

ALTERNATIVE TO A MACHINE-STITCHED ZIPPER

My little hand-picked zipper tutorial on YouTube has had more hits, and comments, than anything else I have put up there. I find this interesting. I was first taught this technique to use when sewing formal wear or difficult-to-handle fabrics, such as velvet or lace. It's a strong way to insert a zipper, practically undetectable and certainly elegant.

It is also super-super-easy to do. My sister Dawn, who has been telling me she can't do zippers for at least 30 years, now uses this method exclusively for all her zippers. I think the appeal of doing zippers this way is that they are done with so much control—slowly, a stitch at a time—with much room to catch and correct any wandering as you go.

1. Sew the seam and leave an opening for the zipper. Press under the seam allowances in the zipper opening.

2. Lay the zipper behind the opening, positioning the middle of the teeth just behind the folded seam allowance. I usually don't pin; I use my hands to keep the zipper in position as I sew. You might prefer pinning.

3. Thread a needle and if you want, pass the thread over a dry bar of soap. Coating the thread like this will keep it from tangling or knotting as you sew.

4. Working from the right side, bring the needle up and then take a tiny stitch backwards. This is called a *prick stitch* (page 167).

5. Bring the needle up again but a little way in front of the first stitch, so there is a gap between stitches. Make another backstitch.

6. Continue in this rhythm until one side of the zipper is sewn.

7. Sew the second side of the zipper the same way.

8. Turn to the inside of the garment and stitch the long edge of the zipper tape to each seam allowance. This can be done with a hand backstitch (page 164) or by machine. Here is a hand-picked zipper from the wrong side, before the reinforcement machine stitches have been made in the seam allowance.

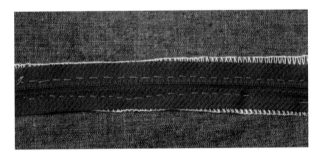

Chapter 7

Sleeves and Cuffs

I am asked about sleeves more than any other area of garment construction. Folks want to know what to do about little pleats in the sleeve cap, sleeves that refuse to ease in, lumpy cuffs, and the dreaded, nearly impossible-to-get-right, continuous lap. I suspect no other area of sewing has sent more seam rippers across the room, or *wadders** into the cupboard, than sleeves, from cap to cuff.

I want to make it clear that a lot of the problems you might be having with your sleeves are a case of, "It's not you, it's them." Not all fabrics are able to ease in easily, that's a fact. Not every sleeve, or fabric, needs the same sleeve cap height. There is no real reason why most cuffs must be made of multiple pattern pieces or why finishing a little slit above a cuff has to be a major construction exercise.

There are simple ways around the sleeve issues. Trust your common sense and feel empowered to work beyond the pattern instructions. Sewists are born problem solvers. Let's apply that to sleeves.

* Wadder: A garment-gone-bad, so disappointing that you want to wad it up and throw it somewhere out of sight …

CONTINUOUS LAP-CUFF OPENINGS

The continuous lap is often used to face cuff openings in women's shirts and blouses. As a technique, it involves ten layers of fabric (garment fabric, placket fabrics, and turn-under of the raw edges) in a short area. As a result, it is hard to make this lap blend into the sleeve. Fortunately, there are variations of the continuous lap that are easy to do and often more attractive.

LOOK FAMILIAR?

Both of these laps are definite _F.A.I.L._s and would frustrate any sewist.

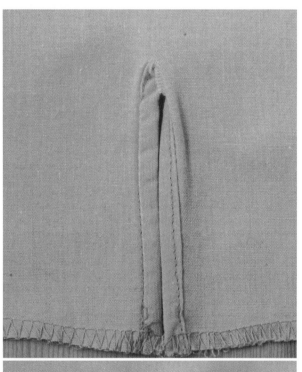

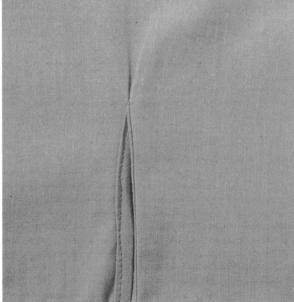

WHY THIS HAPPENS

In the first example, it is clear that the stitching did not quite catch the top edge of the opening when the strip was stitched down, and as result has started to fray away. In the second example, the top of the finished edges of the lap strip were folded and stitched together with a short diagonal seam, as the pattern requested. However, from the outside the results look very bumpy and not at all professional.

FIX IT RIGHT NOW

The lap with a bump at the top could be improved by removing that short seam intended to sew the strips together at the top of the opening. The next step would be to press as smoothly as you can. For the poor lap that didn't quite catch all the facing strip in its stitching, the only real solution is to remove that lap entirely, press, and try one of the other methods described below.

NEXT TIME

Fine-Tuning the Traditional Continuous Lap

1. Press under a small seam allowance on one long edge of the lap piece. (I usually make my lap piece longer than the pattern suggests so I have something to hold onto, and then trim any excess off later.)

2. Slash the sleeve open through the center of the lap placement line on the pattern.

3. Pin the lap strip right sides together to the sleeve along one side of the opening only.

4. Working with the sleeve side facing you, stitch the lap down. There are three tricks to this step that really make a difference:

- **Trick 1:** Sew with the sleeve on top, and the lap strip underneath it, next to the bed of the machine. Typically the part of the seam that misses in stitching is at the top of the sleeve slash—so keep that where you can see it.

- **Trick 2:** Keep the raw edges of the slash and lap strip even until you approach the turn at the top, where it is important to let the lap extend slightly past the edge of the slash. This tactic will make sure that the entire strip is caught in the stitching. Pivot at the top of the placket, take two or three small stitches across the top, pivot, and continue stitching down the other side of the placket.

- **Trick 3:** Cut out a small notch (page 163) in the seam allowance at the point between the pivots after stitching. This will both free up the strip when it turns at the corner so that it won't pucker and removes some of the bulk inside the turn.

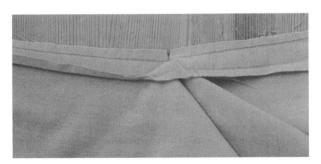

5. Turn the strip to the inside of the sleeve, wrap it over the seam, and sew the remaining edge of the strip just inside the previous stitching line, by hand or by machine.

6. Turn to the right side and press one side of the placket over the other.

7. The usual next step is to sew a little seam across the top of the strips, the method used to produce the _F.A.I.L._

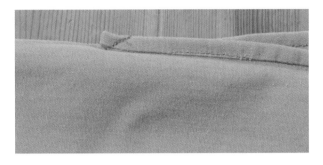

Because it tends to produce _F.A.I.L._s, I don't like doing that little seam at the top. In my world it tends to disappear under the presser foot and emerge crooked, not to mention the lump it leaves under the top of the placket. I prefer to turn the sleeve inside out, fold the sleeve in line with the lap, and sew a small dart from just below the lap opening up into the sleeve for about 2″ (5cm). If you keep the angle of the dart slight, and sort of fade it into the sleeve gradually, this gives a nice subtle ending to the lap, with both sides of the opening folded into the inside.

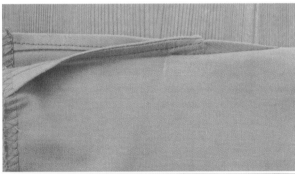

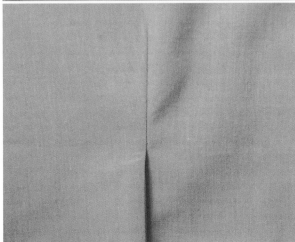

Alternates to the Continuous Lap

If all these bright ideas don't change how you feel about the traditional continuous lap, use one of my less conventional methods, which involve fewer layers and tend to lie more smoothly.

These alternate approaches simply finish the long ends of the slash by hand, machine or even a serger. Once finished, the top of the slit is again hidden in a tiny dart that disappears into the sleeve. So easy to do.

1. Slash the bottom of the sleeve open at the placket cutting line marked on the pattern.

2. Decide on the method you want to use to finish the raw edges of the slash. Whatever method you use, this approach requires that the top of the slit will have more of a U-shape than a straight cut and a tight pivot.

There are three options for finishing these raw edges:

• Roll the edges under with your fingers and hand stitch them.

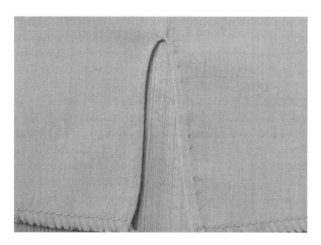

• Make a narrow hem on each side of the cut edge at the machine.

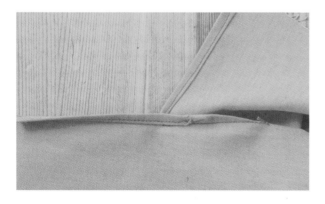

• Feed the cut edge through a serger set up for a rolled hem, with a close stitch length. To do this easily, cut a little curve from the top of the slash so it will be easier to pull the slit straight as it is fed through the serger. If you try to pull a simple cut straight, it is likely you will miss the fabric at that top corner.

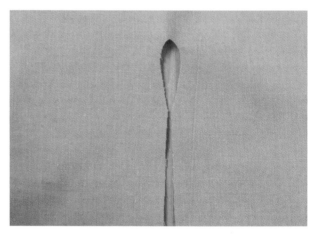

I love the neatness of this finish as well as all that extra fabric bulk that it isn't adding to this little detailed area of the sleeve.

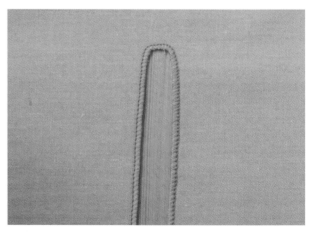

3. To finish, fold the sleeve right sides together with the sides of the slit even. Sew a tiny dart at the top end, starting the dart legs about ¾″ (2cm) below the curved end of the slit. Continue the dart so it is at least 1½″ (4cm) longer, in a gentle angle to blend into the fabric of the sleeve (see Fine-Tuning the Traditional Continuous Lap, Step 7, page 109).

TAILORED SLEEVE PLACKETS

I love, love, love making tailored, men's-style sleeve plackets. They look so complicated but are about 100% easier to make than those conventional continuous laps. The trick is to reconfigure your head about them, and see them as an easy, not complex, sewing task. After all, what's a tailored placket other than just a facing around a cut, and a nice little patch that can be used to hide any potential mistakes. Now don't you feel better?

LOOK FAMILIAR?

This _F.A.I.L._ replicates a placket shown to me by a beginning shirtmaker. The pattern had a two-piece placket. Despite her best efforts, and attempts to follow multiple markings, the underlap peeked out from behind the tower portion of this placket.

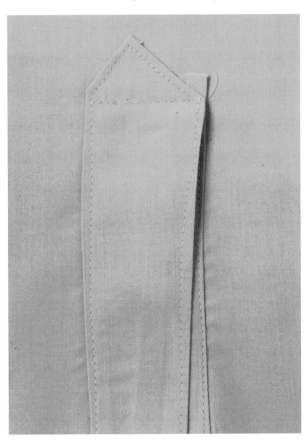

WHY THIS HAPPENS

Using more than one piece to make the placket can result in extra bulk under the tower, which can make topstitching difficult. If your pattern has these two pattern pieces, I suggest you tape them together and cut a single-fabric placket piece that look like the ones that follow (see Make a Placket Template, page 112).

FIX IT RIGHT NOW

The best tactic is to unpick the topstitching, press, and repress from the right side ensuring all parts are tucked in. You have probably anticipated this fix yourself, but really it is your only option. Be cheered that there is an easier way to make shirt plackets

Tip **Getting the Tower Placed Correctly**

For a long time I specialized in getting the "tower" part of the placket facing the wrong direction on my sleeves. Since the construction of these units starts on the wrong side of the garment, it is really easy to get confused. Here's what helped me. The tall, peaked tower part of the placket has to face to the back of the sleeve, and the back of the sleeve is always marked in the cap by double notches. Therefore, to end up facing this direction once the placket is turned to the right side, you have to reverse this in your mind. The placket needs to be pinned, and initially sewn, to the wrong side of the sleeve so the tower is on the front side of the sleeve, which is marked in the cap by a single notch. Does this help? I hope so.

NEXT TIME

Plackets are so much easier when done with one pattern piece and minimal markings. Just take it one step at a time and you will be fine.

The hardest part of making a sleeve placket is not panicking when faced with all the lines for marking, cutting, folding, and stitching on the pattern pieces. I handle this myself by not doing any marking at all. Here is how that works.

Make a Placket Template

1. Trace the sleeve placket pattern piece onto tracing paper. If necessary, tape placket pieces together to make one unit, so it looks like the placket pattern below. Make a mirrored trace for each placket. You will dispose of these once you have stitched through them. If you are working with a PDF pattern, you can print off multiples of the placket pattern piece and use those as your stitch-through templates. I do this a lot.

2. Cut out two placket pieces. Press under a ¼″ (0.5cm) seam allowance on the long side edges and around the tower. It will be necessary to make a small clip in the inner corner of the top of the placket to press around the tower. It is so much easier to do this now by pressing rather than fussing around with the placket once it is sewn to the sleeve.

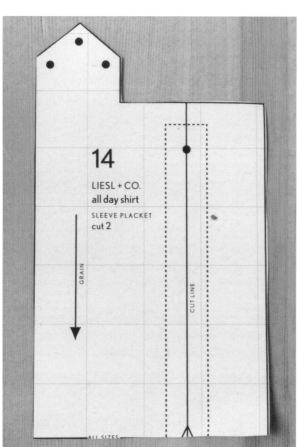

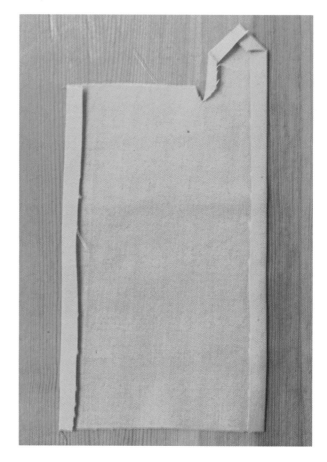

To know where and how much to clip to liberate the seam allowance on the inner angle of the tower, first fold under the ¼″ (0.5cm) and then clip from the corner to the fold. I have drawn that clip line here to show where that would be.

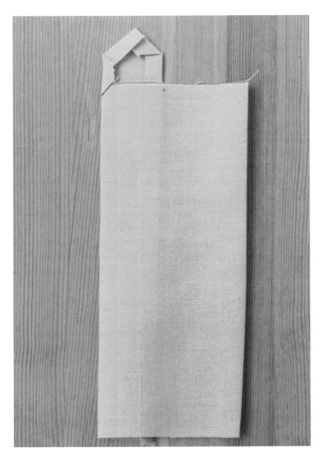

3. Pin each placket piece right side to the wrong side of the sleeve, the tower portion facing the front of the sleeve, and lining up the center of the stitching box with the cutting line marked on the sleeve pattern. Pin the paper tracing over each placket. It might be necessary to unfold the long, pressed edges to situate the paper over the placket piece accurately.

4. Using a smaller-than-normal stitch length to make removing the paper easier, stitch around the box. After stitching, carefully tear the paper away.

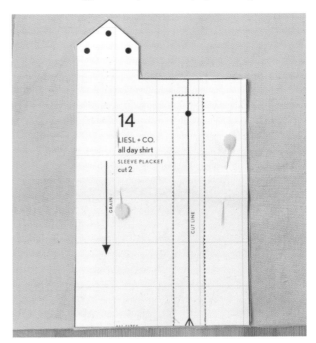

5. Cut right through the center of the stitching box and out to each corner, making a decent-size little wedge, and then press the seam allowance away from the placket opening.

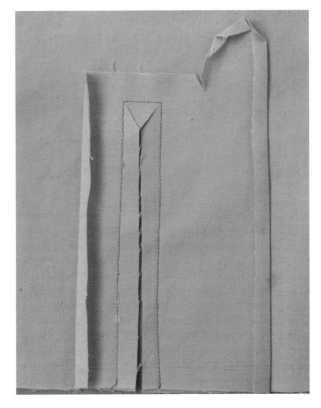

Finish the Placket from the Right Side

1. Pull the placket through to the outside. Check to make sure there are not any puckers at the corners of the box. If there are, go back in and make sure you have clipped right up to each corner.

2. Face the placket underlay by wrapping it around the seam allowance to the right side. Stitch this up to the top of the stitching box, not beyond. Press, ensuring the ends of the underlay are all pressed up and away from the top of the box stitching.

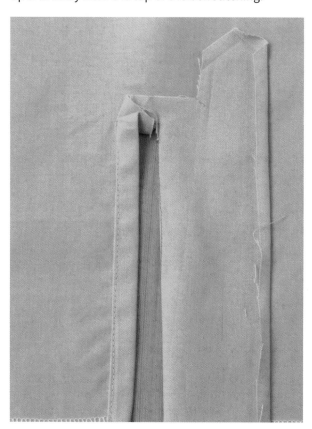

3. Fold the whole tower unit over the placket opening and arrange it so it covers everything neatly. I love doing this part because it is so easy but looks so professional. The tower section essentially becomes a patch that is topstitched over to cover any raw edges at the top of the underlay binding. Trim the ends of the underlay if you need to. Measure the width of the placket all the way up to make sure it is even. Press.

4. Then stitch the tower down in two steps.

A. Edgestitch the inside edge top placket next to the fold, stopping the stitching just even with the top of the opening, keeping the placket underlay out of the way. Don't backstitch but pull the threads to the wrong side of the sleeve and tie off to make it look neater. I have done this below in turquoise thread.

B. Rearrange the placket and pin. Edgestitch the placket up along the outside, pivoting across the "roof" of the tower. You may be worried about a tiny bit of the seam allowance creeping into view as you pivot at the point of the roof. To prevent this, stop at that pivot point, needle down, and use a pin to tuck any stray seam allowance out of the way. Lower the presser foot and then stitch down to meet the previous stitching line at the inner edge of the placket. Pivot and stitch across the top of the opening, through all layers. Pull the threads to the inside and tie off.

This technique can be adapted to other sleeve openings.

• *The placket opening can be made longer than the usual 6˝ (15cm).* These longer plackets are common in casual shirts in which the sleeves might be rolled up—having more room at the wrist opening makes this easier. However, these sleeves usually have a button and buttonhole added to the middle of the placket, so the placket doesn't open up too much when the sleeves are worn down.

• *The width proportions of the placket can be changed.* For example, the conventional 1˝ (2.5cm) finished placket width can be reduced for a more feminine look in women's shirts. I sometimes also do a streamlined narrower and shorter version when making cotton blouses to avoid messing around with the continuous laps. There are no rules, really, and the nice thing about understanding the principles of a technique is that you can then use them in your own way.

SLEEVE CAPS

I feel that the most significant seam sewn in any garment is the one that sets in a sleeve. No matter what else has been done right, a sleeve that is not set in smoothly says homemade, *not handmade*. No matter how beautifully the rest of the garment looks, a rough looking sleeve cap undermines it all.

LOOK FAMILIAR?

This *F.A.I.L.* needs no introduction, we have all had sleeves turn out like this.

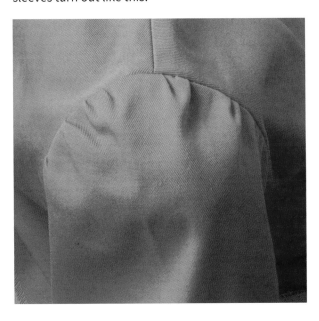

WHY THIS HAPPENS

Many things are going on here and all those issues, and how to get ahead of them, are discussed in detail. It is worth noting that all the nonpuffy set-in sleeves shown as samples in this section were made with the same pattern. So, what went particularly wrong with this sleeve?

Fabric. Not all fabrics have enough built-in ease to really ease. Read that one again. It took me so long to figure this out. The tactics shared here will help set in any sleeve, but before you start to sew make sure that you have a fabric that is working with you and not against you. The fabric in this sleeve is a cotton twill, midweight, and inflexible. It simply doesn't have enough inherent give to ease well. A fabric like this asks to be used in a raglan style, or a more casual, dropped sleeve style in which little easing is required.

FIX IT RIGHT NOW

The only answer is to take this sleeve out, press it flat, and try again with the methods that follow.

Before you tackle any sleeve setting issues, consider several background factors and circumstances. With sleeves, context is everything.

What Kind of Sleeve Is It?

Two types of sleeves use a seam near the shoulder. These are the classic set-in sleeve and the shirt-style sleeve.

• A **set-in sleeve** is cut high under the arm and close to the body. In this sleeve style, the shoulder seam lies near the end of the natural shoulder. Extra fabric at the top of the sleeve is eased to make a curved cap, which helps the sleeve travel over the round top of the shoulder and past the shoulder joint. A high, round sleeve cap is apparent on any sleeve pattern piece. A set-in sleeve should hang off the shoulder smoothly and without wrinkles because of the shaped cap.

• A **shirt sleeve** has a wider, much shallower sleeve cap. This sleeve usually is combined with some version of a dropped shoulder seam. The wider sleeve and dropped seam give this more casual sleeve some extra room and comfort.

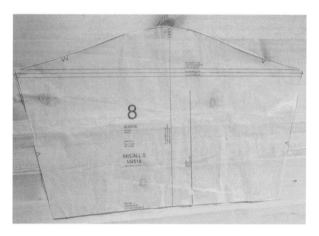

Note, however—*and this is really, really important*—a shirt sleeve with a shorter cap will always tend to have some vertical folds. Don't wear yourself out trying to fix these folds. They come with the design.

The Fabric Is Everything

A successfully set-in sleeve absolutely requires a fabric with some malleability. My dream fabric for set-in sleeves would be a slightly loose wool flannel. My nightmare fabric would be silk dupioni. Wool flannel likes heat, steam, and molding. Dupioni resists this kind of shaping with every fiber it has. Consider and respect your fabric. Rethink your pattern choice if you have to. Maybe switch out that tight, high sleeve for your mother-of-the-bride dress for one with raglan seams or with intended pleats in the sleeve cap. Being smart about fabric and patterns will head off much sleeve-setting angst.

It is helpful to consider that different parts of a sleeve cap will have different potential for easing than others, and honor that too. For instance, it is always more possible to ease the sleeve cap in along the sides, where the grain moves to the bias, than along the top few inches right at the top of the sleeve cap where everything is on grain. My advice is to not even try to ease the very top of a sleeve, and instead focus on pulling up those easing threads on either side of it instead.

Don't Be Afraid to Alter Sleeve Cap Height

Sometimes I reduce the height of a sleeve cap—sometimes because I decide the cap provided in the pattern is too high and sometimes to compensate for a fabric with a bit of rigidity.

Here are some guidelines for assessing sleeve cap heights, but first measure the circumference of the armhole. Do this by overlaying the shoulder seam stitching lines of the front and back pattern pieces and measure with a vertical tape measure laid on the stitching lines.

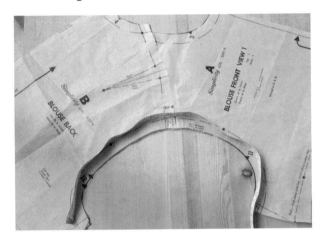

Compare this measure to one taken along the stitching line of the sleeve cap. As a general rule:

- A tightly woven, less ease-friendly fabric should not have a sleeve-cap measurement more than 1″ (2.5cm) longer than the armhole measurement.

- A more ease-friendly, loosely woven fabric should have a sleeve-cap measurement about 1½″ (4cm) longer than the armhole measurement.

It is often suggested to reduce sleeve cap height by just lowering the seamline at the top of the cap.

I used to do this, but I found that this method tended to really distort the shape, and comfort, of the sleeve. Reducing the length of the sleeve cap seam evenly with slashing and overlapping does a better job of shrinking that cap but keeps the original sleeve design.

1. Cut horizontally across the sleeve pattern at the top of the sleeve, just below where the cap starts to curve.

2. Figure out how much cap you need to remove. Divide it into ¼″ (0.5cm) sections. This number is how many overlaps you will need to make. So if ¾″ (1.5cm) is how much you want to remove, make three slashes, evenly spaced, from the top of the sleeve caps to just a whisper above the cut line (cuts 1, 2, 3). Overlap the pattern a ¼″ (0.5cm) at the top of each of these slashes, tapering to the original sleeve width by the time you meet the cut. Once you have adjusted the top of the sleeve, rejoin it to the original lower sleeve. It will probably be necessary to redraw the sleeve seams slightly to bring them in line with the new cap.

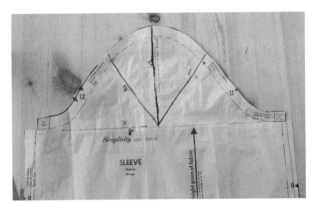

Rethink the Easing Stitches

We all put machine basting stitches in the top of the sleeve to pull up and ease the cap into a smaller shape. I want to share a trick—put the two rows of basting so they straddle the seam stitching line, not above it. Doing this will make sure the easing can be held still during the stitching, and makes it far less likely to form those little pleaty things. The line of basting that shows after final stitching can be removed. The turquoise stitches are the basting stitches. Note that I have placed the line of stitches that will be removed closer to the stitching line for more control.

Tip A Case for Three Basting Lines

Interestingly, many vintage garments with fine fabrics and set-in sleeves use three, not two, lines of gathering for greater control. A real lesson there.

Shape

This is important. Pressing into shape can happen only before a detail/section is sewn into the garment, not afterward. This applies to under-collars (see Option 1: My Own Variation on the One-Giant-Seam Method, Step 1, page 46) and to sleeve caps. Work at the end of an ironing board to shape a sleeve cap.

1. Sew and press the shoulder and side seams. Measure around the unfinished armhole.

2. Carefully ease around the sleeve cap, pulling in the ease stitches. Make sure that the very top section (see above) is not eased, focusing on the front and back portions of the sleeve. Stop easing when the sleeve measurement matches the armhole measurement.

3. Hang the sleeve off the end of ironing board, almost as if the board were a shoulder. Shoot steam into the shoulder cap and work with it with your hands, until all the easing has turned into a nice smooth, rounded cap. Leave the sleeve hanging and let it cool.

4. Sew the sleeve into the armhole. Trim the sleeve seam allowance below the sleeve notches only. Do not try to press this lower section of the sleeve; let it sit naturally up into the armhole. Leave the seam allowances as is above the notches and press these toward the sleeve. I usually zigzag over this untrimmed seam allowance to stiffen it, creating a sort of low-key sleeve head. See more on those in Supporting the Sleeve Cap.

Supporting the Sleeve Cap

The 90s and giant shoulder pads are over, but the issue of support to the top of a sleeve cap is still worth talking about. In the more substantial sleeves of jackets and coats in particular, strategies to keep the sleeve cap from collapsing as it drops from the shoulder seam are really helpful. Supporting and maintaining the cup of the sleeve as it goes over the shoulder can make a huge difference Here are some simple ideas.

OPTION 1: PARTIALLY INTERFACE THE CAP AREA

I do this a lot, using a fusible knit interfacing. I like using a knit fusible because it tends not to change the hand of the outer fabric but keeps the line of the sleeve over the shoulder and upper arm. Fused-on support is an excellent technique for midweight soft fabrics like the rayon damask shown here. If the fabric has a harder surface (such as a gabardine), I would pink the bottom edges of the interfacing to blend it in.

OPTION 2: ADD A SLEEVE HEAD

This technique works well for fabrics such as wool that have body but may need some lift out from the shoulder before the sleeve drops to the arm. Most coats and jacket sleeves benefit from this kind of support. The sleeve head I use most often is a strip of something soft (such as polyester microfleece or a bonded batting such as needle punch) sewn over the seam allowance of the shoulder seam, from notch to notch, with the head next to the sleeve. As a process, I generally like to sew a strip about 1″–1½″ (2.5–4cm) wide to the seam allowance, try the garment on, and trim to fit. I usually end up with a sort of elongated half-moon shape like this:

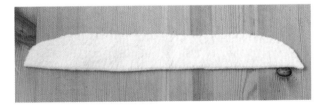

Here is the sleeve with that head from the outside. You can see how the head keeps the top of the sleeve from collapsing.

And here is the inside of the sleeve.

In dressy garments with a gathered or puffed sleeve cap, use tulle—the fine netting used in bridal veils—to make fabulous, soft but supportive sleeve heads. Just cut a circle of tulle, fold it in half, gather the raw edges and pull the gathering tight.

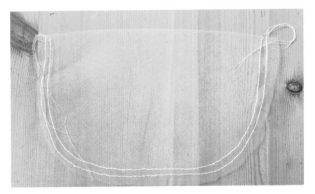

Sew this unit to the sleeve seam allowance by hand or machine, under the seam allowance, so the head is next to the sleeve. Here is what the gathered head looks like sewn inside the sleeve.

And the extra puff as seen from the outside of the sleeve.

Tip Ease-Plussing

A great technique for malleable fabrics, such as wool flannel, particularly with sleeve caps that require little easing, is an old technique called *ease-plussing*. To ease-plus a sleeve, simply stitch a few rows of standard stitching between the notches, with your fingers behind the presser foot holding it back so it piles up behind the foot. Impeding the exit of the fabric this way will naturally build in a slight gather.

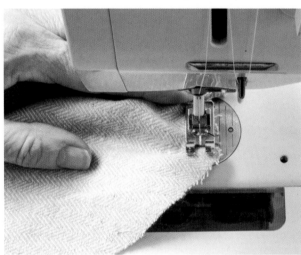

CUFFS

There is not too much to a cuff—in most cases just two rectangles of fabric—but still they are one of those garment-finishing details that can either look finely made or homemade. The main challenges of cuffs are the many layers of fabric and interfacing intersecting in the small space of the sleeve opening and the cuff. It is interesting how difficult it can be to fit the two rectangles together.

In this _F.A.I.L._, the seam allowances peek out at the juncture of the cuff and placket and the topstitched folded upper cuff has slipped away from the cuff stitching line.

The bulk of the multiple layers is very difficult to tuck into the cuff at this busy intersection, even with pinning and basting, and under the movement of the machine.

Hate to say it, but your best bet is to unpick the topstitching, press, and try the method described below.

There are several changes you can make to either the pattern pieces or the construction methods to produce smoother, cleaner cuffs.

Option 1: Rethink Interfacing

Rather than interface only one layer of the cuff, interface both layers. This might mean switching to a lighter-weight interfacing since you are doubling up support. An interfaced piece will always be more stable than one that is not. Sending both sides of the cuff to the job in the same state will make fitting them together, without puckers, so much easier.

Option 2: Reduce Bulk

The typical cuff has at least one buttonhole and substantial topstitching. Both these details can get tricky over changes in elevation due to fabric layers. Get ahead of this by changing up the pattern to reduce unnecessary seams.

• For a rectangular cuff with straight seams, eliminate one of the long seams by placing that stitching line on the fold, producing a single piece cuff like this one.

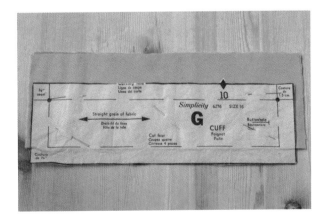

• Also consider switching one of the side seams to one in the middle of the under cuff. This change makes it much easier to sew buttonholes in thicker fabrics. During layout, maintain the top seam but lay the stitching line of one short side at a fold, producing one long cuff piece.

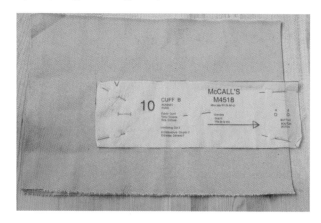

Sew this one short seam, center it in the under cuff, and then sew the top cuff seam. Note how switching the seams like this produces very smooth cuffs with little bulk—perfect for sewing buttonholes!

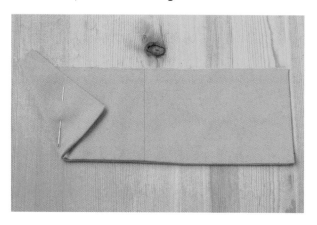

Option 3: Topstitch from the Right Side

In nearly every pattern I have seen, the advice is to sew the sides and the top of the cuff pieces together and then to sew the top cuff, right sides together, to the sleeve. It is then suggested to topstitch the raw edge of the under cuff into place. This was the method used in the *F.A.I.L.*

It is far more effective, and relaxing, to sew the cuffs to the sleeves with a "bagging" technique. This is easiest with a one-piece cuff but also can be used with a two-piece cuff such as those needed for cuffs with a curved shape.

THE ONE-PIECE CUFF OPTION

1. Sew the right side of one edge of the cuff to the wrong side of the sleeve.

2. Fold the cuff along the top fold line, right sides together. Pin the two halves of the cuff together, with the sleeve sandwiched between them. Stitch the short ends of each cuff, tucking the sleeve out of the way so it won't catch. Pivot at the corner (feel for the edge of the placket with your hand so you will know when to turn) and stitch about 1″ (2.5cm) over the previous stitching made when one edge of the cuff was sewn to the seam. See the turquoise stitching below. I don't actually measure this. I just sew for a bit, leaving a nice big gap in the stitching. You can do this in two short seams instead of pivoting, of course, if that makes it easier for you to wrap the cuff around the sleeve.

3. Trim the seam allowances, turn, and press.

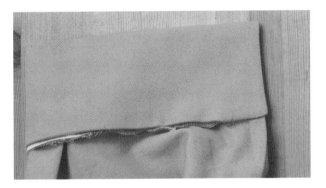

The right side of the sleeve it will look like this. Tuck the remaining seam allowances in at the top.

4. To finish, pin and then topstitch around all edges of the cuff.

THE TWO-PIECE CUFF OPTION

1. Sew one cuff to the sleeve, right side of the cuff to the wrong side of the sleeve.

2. Pin the upper cuff to the lower cuff, with the sleeve sandwiched between them, right sides together, all raw edges even, tucking the sleeve out of the way so it doesn't catch. Stitch the short ends of each cuff together, beginning about 1″ (2.5cm) in from the corner along the top cuff seamline, pivoting and stitching along the short ends of the cuff, pivoting and sewing over the previous stitching line at the cuff seam for another 1″ (2.5cm). See the turquoise stitching lines below.

3. Now the interesting part. Turn the cuff to the right side and press. Reach down through the unstitched top of the cuff to the seams inside. Pin both cuffs together, the sleeve between them, raw edges even. Stitch over the previous stitching line to close the bottom of the cuff.

4. Turn the cuff to the right side again and press. Tuck the remaining seam allowances in the gap at the top of the cuff and pin. Topstitch around all edges of the cuff.

Chapter 8

Buttonholes and Buttons

Raise your hand if sewing buttonholes is your favorite part of the garment making process. What? No hands?

I am not surprised. Making buttonholes feels high risk. Who doesn't feel anxious at the thought of messing up those tiny, hard-to-remove stitches? Who doesn't dread that slash-it-open moment? Who hasn't un-picked and redone buttonholes nearly every other one, or cut right through the satin stitches just when you thought you were done?

The truth is buttonholes are just not a one-size-fits-all situation. A buttonhole that works well on a cotton shirt is likely too heavy for a silk blouse. The same type of buttonhole also may get stuck when you try to stitch it on that nice coating. Great reliable buttonholes require good strategy as much as careful execution.

Fortunately, we sewists have a few tricks up our sleeves, and whatever the layers throw at us, we can deal with it. Relax. I absolutely know any sewist can produce beautiful buttonholes without angst. Here are the tactics that will get you through.

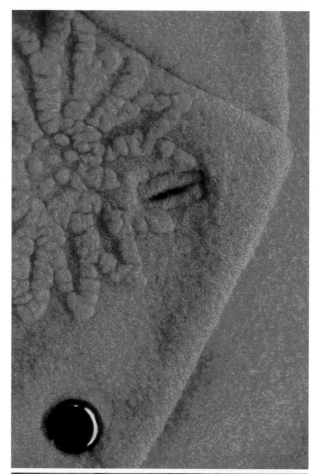

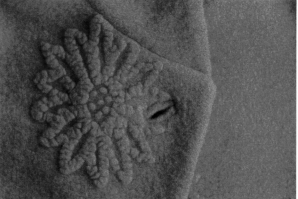

MACHINE BUTTONHOLES

The buttonhole on the left has a completely different stitch quality on each side. The buttonhole in the middle has sides, called *beads*, so close together that it would be impossible to slash it open without cutting through the stitches. The "automatic" buttonhole on the right has sides of unequal length.

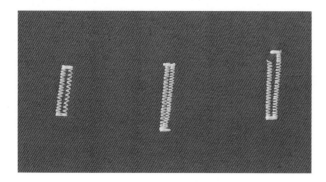

WHY THIS HAPPENS

- **Buttonhole on the left:** The difference in stitch quality in the sides is possible in any buttonhole that stitches forward for one side and backward in the other. Machines always stitch more efficiently forward than in reverse. Some machines deal with this by straight stitching back to the beginning after the first bead is stitched.

- **Buttonhole in the middle:** If there is insufficient interfacing/stabilizer under the buttonhole, the dense rows of stitching can pull too close together. Or it can be a machine issue. I once had a top-of-the-line machine that didn't allow me to widen the cutting area. I gave this machine to my daughter, who uses it to hem curtains.

- **Buttonhole on the right:** Sides of uneven length generally reflect a machine that works a little harder sewing in one direction than the other, so some stitches pack up. Sewing over a layer of paper/stabilizer can help. I have noticed that this issue can occur in computerized buttonholes that "count stitches" on each side—not too useful when layers or direction change.

FIX IT RIGHT NOW

If you notice differences in the buttonhole sides when the fabric is still under the foot, it may be possible to just go around the buttonhole again. If this works, you are lucky. More than likely you will need to turn the fabric over, use a seam ripper to slice through the satin stitches, and unpick the whole thing. Tweezers are helpful. So is a glass of wine. Press to close up the stitching holes before you try again

NEXT TIME

Check Your Thread

For messy stitches, the first thing to change is your thread. All cotton threads give good coverage. And I always loosen the upper tension dial so the lock stitch is pulled to the underside of the fabric for a nice, smooth satin-stitch surface.

Use Spray Starch

When working with fine fabrics, I always, always spray starch the fabric in the buttonhole area. This makes an enormous difference in preventing the two sides of heavy zigzagging from pulling together toward the middle of the buttonhole.

Tip Dealing with a Bulky Buttonhole Foot

In some cases, a buttonhole foot or attachment is too bulky for a detailed area (like at the end of a collar band). If I suspect that my buttonhole foot will catch over the layers, I replace it with an appliqué presser foot. This foot has a cut-out area on the bottom to let dense satin stitches move through. I find the DIY method works best for these collar band buttonholes. For neatness, I usually don't cut this buttonhole open.

Ditch the Automatic ... DIY Instead

Doing buttonhole-making yourself may seem like a lot of trouble. But isn't it more trouble to unpick a bunch of *F.A.I.L.* buttonholes? With DIY, you set the density and width of the buttonhole sides and the bars at the end so the cutting area is adjusted for fabric weight. And since both sides are sewn in the same direction, they always look the same.

DIY BUTTONHOLE:
MARK

Mark the starting and end point of each buttonhole. For a guide, I mark a strip of masking tape and press it next to the buttonhole area.

DETERMINE THE MACHINE SETTINGS

Figure out the stitch density (set by stitch length) and stitch width for the sides of the buttonhole you find attractive. A finer fabric will require a lighter button-hole with narrower beads, a narrower cutting area, and more space between the satin stitches. Bulkier fabrics really need wide, dense beads and a wider cutting area for bigger buttons. Experiment with the settings and your fabric, and make a note of the stitch width and length settings.

SEW THE BUTTONHOLE

1. Set the stitch width for the sides of the button-hole. I used a close stitch length (between 1 to 0), the sides set at 2.0 width. The bar tacks at the end were set at 4.0.

2. Sew the left side first. At the end of this run, stop with the needle down on the inside edge of the row of stitching. Change the width setting for the bar tacks.

3. Carefully turn the wheel by hand to see how wide the bar tack swing is. Realign the fabric so the left swing of the needle goes right into the outer, left side of the satin stitches. I usually make the bar tack by turning the hand wheel myself about three times—I don't like a bulky tack. End with the needle down on the right side of the swing of the stitch.

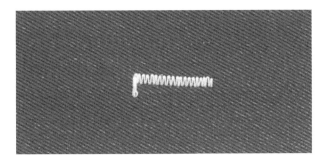

4. Raise the presser foot and pivot the work to stitch the other side going forward. Lower the presser foot. Raise the needle.

5. Change the stitch-width setting back to a narrower width. Turn the hand wheel and observe how the needle swings side to side. Working by eye, slightly adjust the fabric so the left swing of the needle drops exactly down into the outer left side of the bar tack. Stitch the second side of the buttonhole. To keep both sides parallel, I find it helps to line up the previ-ous row of stitching with a spot on the presser foot.

6. Raise the needle and change the width setting back to the stitch width for the final bar tack. Turn the hand wheel to see where the needle will land and move the fabric over so the left swing of the needle drops exactly down on the left, outer edge of the second side of the buttonhole. Stitch the bar tack. Tie off. Pull the threads to the wrong side and tie or begin and end with a few straight stitches set at 0 stitch length.

Vintage Buttonholers

If all you've read up to now sounds like too much work, and all you really want are perfect button-holes that better than your current machine makes, I have only two words to say—vintage buttonholers. Nothing does a better job, nothing. I find vintage buttonholers particularly good for heavier fabrics, tailoring, or for fine fabrics. I also find their round-ended buttonholes beautiful.

Can They Be Used on Your Machine?

Older buttonholers have a short, straight shank and can fit modern machines that have these. Some, but not most, of the later models from the 1960s are designed only for slant shanks, like those on the Singer Slant-O-Matic and Rocketeer. Before you buy any vintage attachment, make sure you have a machine that it will fit. I have tried them on a wide variety of machines and have had trouble attaching them only to machines with a built-in walking foot like the Pfaff. The old buttonholers, however, do seem to fit most comfortably on older machines and you might consider having one of these dedicated to buttonhole making. As for the attachments, I have bought mine on eBay and in thrift shops and have never paid more than five dollars for any of them.

How the Templates Work

Vintage buttonholers operate by templates.

These metal templates are used in the wide variety of short-shank buttonholers.

These plastic templates are used in both the short shank and slant shank buttonholers produced by Singer in the 1960s.

Templates control the movement of the attachment under the needle in a pretty nonnegotiable way. That's why they are able to make such incredibly precise and consistent buttonholes. The templates are loaded either into the bottom or top of the units.

Two buttonholers that load from the bottom, as seen from the top

And from the bottom with the template doors open

A newer 60s buttonholer from the top

And with the template door open

To use either version, you must cover the feed dogs. In most cases this is done by covering them with a plate screwed on to the bed of the machine, included with the attachment. In many slant needle machines, the throat plate itself can be raised by a lever to cover the feed dogs. All versions of the buttonholers allow for adjustments to stitch density, bead width, and cutting space. All do a variety of keyhole and round-ended buttonholes. The newer 60s models also have fantastic templates for stitching the first stage of bound buttonholes. Because there are so many possible combinations of stitch density, bead size, and cutting spaces possible I suggest you stitch off as many of these as you can for reference.

Here are some of my own samples.

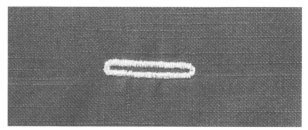

A close-up of a wonderful, rounded-end buttonhole, stitched around twice with cotton machine embroidery thread for great coverage

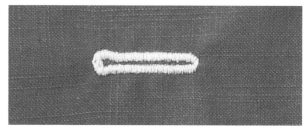

A keyhole buttonhole

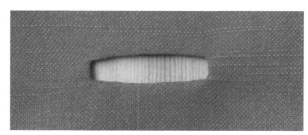

First step of a buttonhole made with the bound-buttonhole template. The rest of this buttonhole would be completed by using either the windowpane or lips method described in the next section.

BOUND BUTTONHOLES

When dealing with heavy, delicate, or textured fabrics, a machine-made buttonhole can be both difficult to do and inappropriate for the fabric. In these situations, a bound buttonhole may be the only sensible, and surprisingly most stress-free, option. I find making bound buttonholes a relaxing process. However, I use only easy methods.

Tip The Benefit of Hand Stitching

You will notice I often suggest that small, careful areas in construction are done with hand stitches, rather than by machine. There is good reason for this. Handmade stitches are easy to correct as you work. The most crucial areas of stitching, such as across the tiny ends of a bound buttonhole, for example, can get lost and out of control under a machine presser foot. Core Skills (page 162) explains the most useful stitches used in construction.

LOOK FAMILIAR?

Bound buttonholes should look elegant. Ones like this *F.A.I.L.* can look lumpy, uneven, and gape open.

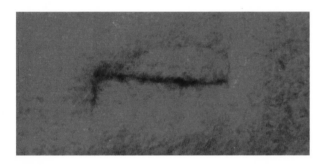

WHY THIS HAPPENS

This is bulky fabric. And there are many layers and a lot of sewing activity in very tight spaces here. I counted ten layers of fabric, including seam allowances, in an area roughly 1½″ × ½″ (4 × 1cm). Where's all that fabric supposed to go? Additionally, much of the stitching is done from the wrong side. I call this the presto-change method—a hopeful approach that no matter what happened on the wrong side of the fabric, everything will look just fine when it is turned over. Rarely happens.

FIX IT RIGHT NOW

I wish I had a miracle cure to share. I don't. If your bound buttonholes are really messed up, I suggest finding really big, flashy buttons and keeping the garment done up. Alternately you can sew some big snaps over the buttonholes and lap the opposite side over. Consider this a contribution to the discourse on gender, and not a way to hide a mistake.

NEXT TIME

There are two easy ways to make bound buttonholes: the windowpane method (next page) and the lips method (page 134). I have refined these processes to make them even easier. Here are my favorite tricks.

- Mark the paper, not the fabric. Yes, I know the books and online tutorials show a lot of precise thread marking, but it is so much easier and more accurate to make the placement marks on tracing paper and just stitch through it.

- Start by working with single, large pieces of fabric laid over the garment to make the buttonhole boxes and then trim it into sections. Since none of us have hands like Barbie, this is so much easier than trying to manipulate tiny squares.

- Do as much as you can from the right, not the wrong, side of the garment. Seeing the end product and working backward is always helpful.

- When working with very heavy fabrics, like the coat at the beginning of this chapter, I sometimes use a fine, starched knit fabric rather than a woven for the buttonhole facing. Knits don't fray and they stretch easily around the openings without puckering and extra bulk.

Preliminary Steps

PREP THE GARMENT

1. Interface the garment under the buttonhole area. In many coats and jackets, the fronts will already be fully fused with interfacing, so that takes care of that. Alternately, iron a strip of interfacing the full length of the buttonhole area to the wrong side of the front piece. I also interface the button side front, to support the stress of the buttons.

2. Decide on the size of the buttonhole opening. The easiest way to do this is to make a cut in a scrap of interfaced fabric and slide the button through it. In coats and jackets that go over other garments, buttonholes are always horizontal to build in a slight ease of movement.

3. Think about button placement. As a general rule, the size of the button influences the distance from the finished front edge. A larger button may need to be further from the finished edge.

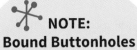

**NOTE:
Bound Buttonholes**

All bound buttonholes should be made in the garment front pieces before any other construction starts.

MARK THE PAPER

1. Draw two buttonhole placement lines parallel to the front edge—one to mark where the buttonholes should start, and one where they should end. Next, make horizontal lines, evenly spaced, for each buttonhole.

2. Draw in the buttonhole stitching boxes, each box as long as the space between the vertical start and stop lines and as wide as the two lips are in proportion to the fabric—less for finer fabrics, more for bulkier fabrics.

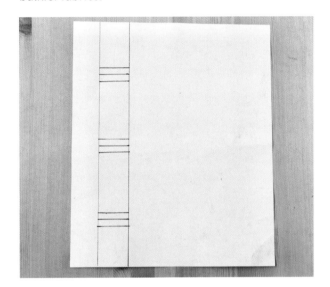

Windowpane Method (Light to Medium Fabric)

This method uses the garment fabric for both the button lips and facing. It works well for linens, wool gabardine, and flannels.

1. Right sides together, pin a strip of garment fabric to the buttonhole area. This strip should be about 4″ (10cm) wide and the length of the buttonhole area. This strip must be absolutely on grain, so the buttonholes lie flat and smooth.

2. Pin the marked paper over the fabric. Make sure the vertical line marking the end of the buttonhole boxes is completely parallel to the front edge of the garment.

3. Stitch around each buttonhole box right through the paper and both layers of fabric. Using a short stitch length, 1.5–2.0, start stitching at the middle of one long side of a buttonhole box, not at the corners as this may weaken them.

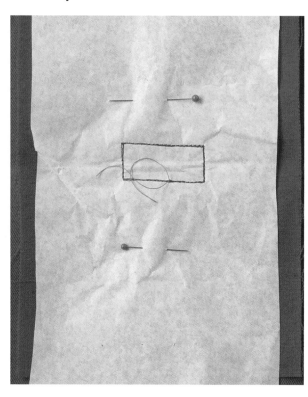

4. Remove the marking paper. Because the stitches are small, it should remove very easily.

5. Cutting through both layers of fabric, slash down the center of each buttonhole and out to the corners. Place a pin at the corners to avoid cutting past the stitching. Be sure to leave a decent-size triangle at the end.

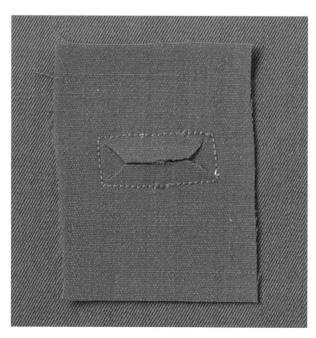

6. Trim away the long fabric strip between each buttonhole to about 1″ (2.5cm) around each box.

MAKE THE BUTTONHOLE LIPS

1. Pull the fabric through the opening to the wrong side. Tug at the triangles of fabric at the end of the box until the box lies flat. If there are puckers at the corners, go back and make sure you have clipped right to the corners. Press the window flat.

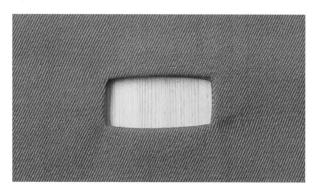

2. On the wrong side of the garment, press the seam allowances of the long side of the box up, extending the crease along the length of the patch.

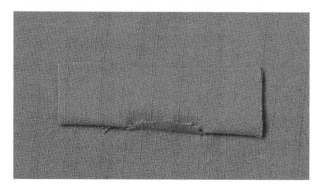

When you have done this to both sides, it will look like a little box pleat behind the window.

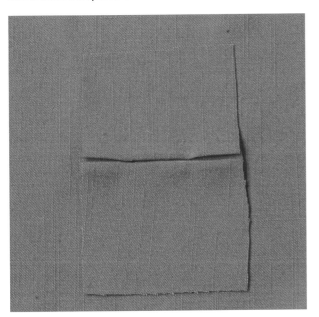

3. Working from the right side of the garment, arrange the fabric of the patch behind the window to form the lips of the buttonhole. Fuss around with this until the lips are the same size and meet evenly in the center of the box. Slip baste (page 168) the lips together and press.

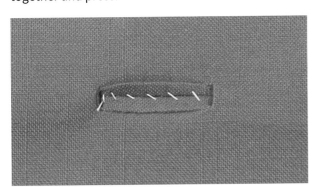

4. Working from the right side, prick stitch (page 167) by hand around the long sides of the buttonhole, burying the stitches in-the-ditch of the previous stitching. If you want, you can carefully machine stitch the edges to the tiny seam allowance of the long sides of the window. I usually don't bother. I feel that the prick stitch is reinforcement enough.

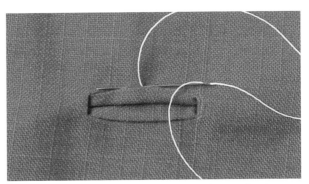

Even though I used white thread, the stitches are hard to see in the well of the seam.

5. Return to the wrong side and, using a zipper foot, stitch the raw edges of the lips together across the ends. You also could do this by hand with a small backstitch (page 164).

**CLEAN UP AND MAKE BUTTONHOLE OPENINGS
IN THE FACING**

Continue constructing the garment. Behind each buttonhole, you will need to make a corresponding opening in the facing. A simple option for most fabrics is to make another faced rectangular opening for the back of each buttonhole. The key is accurate marking, so the buttonhole and facing openings match. Not hard to do.

1. Using four pins for each buttonhole, push the pins from the front of the fabric right through into the facing. Working from the facing side, place a pin at each of the corners for the facing stitching boxes.

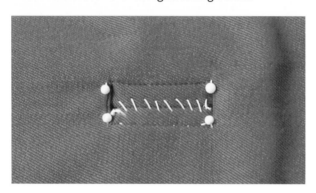

2. When you have completed the facing buttonholes, hand slipstitch the edges of the facing windows to the back of the bound buttonhole openings and you are done.

Tip Easier Option for Nonfraying Fabrics

When working with very bulky and nonfraying fabric like the boiled wool used in the red coat at the beginning of this chapter, it is not necessary to make these formal rectangular finished openings in the facing. In cases like this, I usually just slash the facing behind each buttonhole, turn under the raw edges and slipstitch into place.

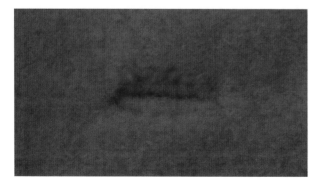

Lips Method (Medium to Heavy Fabrics)

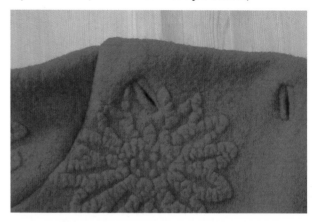

The lips method is better for coatings, meltons, or boiled wools. It uses a lighter fabric or knit for the buttonhole facing and the heavier garment fabric for the buttonhole lips.

I find this approach even easier than the windowpane method. The buttonhole openings are faced, and the buttonhole lips are made separately and then inserted behind the opening. If the garment fabric is heavy, the buttonhole facing can be made with lighter fabric. There are two distinct construction stages in this method, so there's nice room for pauses and corrections.

1. Interface the fronts as described in the Windowpane Method (page 131).

2. Cut the facing fabric about 4″ (10cm) wide and the length of the buttonhole area. It can be self-fabric, a lighter fabric, or even a knit, which I used when sewing the buttonholes for the red coat (photo, page 125).

3. Pin the strip of facing fabric, right sides together, to the buttonhole area of the front piece.

4. Pin the marked tracing paper over the facing fabric. See the Windowpane Method.

5. Stitch and cut open and press the buttonhole boxes just as you would have in the windowpane method. Trim the facing to about 1″ (2.5cm) around each buttonhole box.

MAKE THE BUTTONHOLE LIPS

1. Cut two long strips of on-grain garment fabric about 3″ (8cm) wide and 18″ (46cm) long. I always find it easier to have lots to handle and trim it down afterward.

2. Crease the center of each strip. Right sides together, place the strips with the creases aligned. Using a long machine-basting stitch, stitch down the crease through both layers.

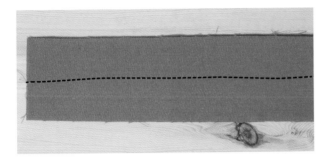

3. Cut this strip into segments about 2½″ (6cm) long, one for each buttonhole. Fold the fabric away from the stitching line, making two lips. Press.

4. Place a set of lips behind each buttonhole opening. Working from the right side, arrange the buttonhole segments so the stitched line is centered in the opening.

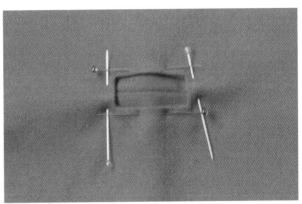

Pin all layers to position. Baste close to the edges of the window.

5. Working one side at a time, fold back the garment to expose the buttonhole window seam allowances along the long sides. Use a zipper foot to get in close and restitch along the stitching lines through all layers.

6. Fold the fabric to expose the tiny triangles at the end of the buttonhole. Again, using a zipper foot stitch through all layers through the triangles, as is done in the windowpane method.

If you are more comfortable with hand stitching, both Steps 5 and 6 can be done by hand rather than at the machine.

7. Continue with construction and make openings in the facing behind each buttonhole as described above.

BUTTONHOLES IN KNITS

LOOK FAMILIAR?

This _F.A.I.L._ buttonhole has a nickname—the dreaded fish mouth. No other explanation necessary.

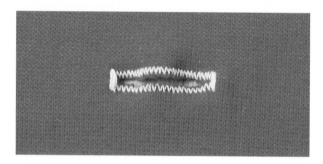

WHY THIS HAPPENS

There is a lot of mechanical activity going on when a machine stitches a buttonhole. With an emotional fabric like a knit, always ready to get stretched out of shape, this process tends to ripple the buttonhole even before it leaves the machine. Once the buttonhole is in use, the stretching out continues. We even see this in ready-to-wear.

FIX IT RIGHT NOW

I would love to say there is a quick fix for the old fish mouth. But there isn't, or at least not a quick one. I have ironed fusible knit interfacing behind a buttonhole like this and hand whipped stitched the edges of the buttonhole to the interfacing. That was a help but not a huge fix.

NEXT TIME

The good news is that issues of gaping buttonholes are easy to see coming and head off. Here are your options:

- Forget the idea of buttonholes all together. Sew on or apply snaps. Of the press-in snaps, I find that KAMsnaps work best.

- Interface the buttonhole area well with a fusible knit interfacing. Be careful to have the nonstretchy direction of the interfacing (this runs parallel to the selvage) in line with the sides of the buttonhole.

- Lay a fabric stabilizer, such as tissue paper, tear-away, or wash-away (my preference), under the fabric before you make the buttonholes.

- Make a corded buttonhole (best choice in my opinion).

- Use one of your machine's built-in stretch button-holes if you have that option. I find these button-holes work best with a stabilizer under them.

Corded Buttonhole

1. Fit the cord into the buttonhole foot. Fold a length of heavy thread, perle cotton, or even dental floss in half and loop it around the hook at the back of the foot. Pull both strands to the front, under the foot, and up on either side of the post, between the two tiny hooks at the front of the foot.

Tip **When Without, Improvise**

I made the sample below when I was in self-isolation due to the COVID-19 pandemic and didn't have any white heavy thread, so I improvised with dental floss. It worked well, although it still smells a bit minty, and I decided to leave it in here. I feel it's part of the historical record of that time and also consistent with my belief that in sewing, ingenuity is everything.

The next trick is to hold both ends of the cord up high so it won't slip out as you stitch. This is how the cord looks once it has been placed in the foot, from the top and from the bottom.

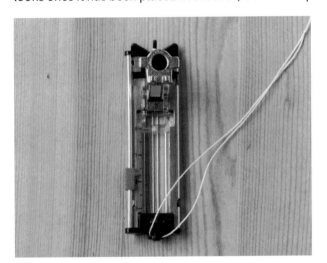 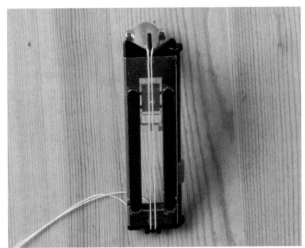

2. Stitch the buttonhole as usual, holding the cord up and taut. When the buttonhole is done, carefully remove the fabric from the machine.

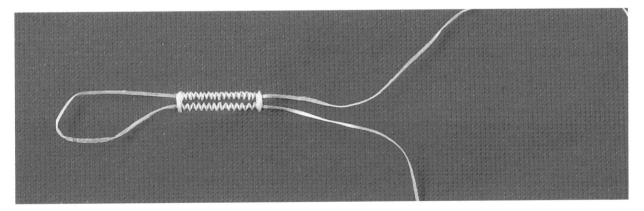

3. Pull on the free ends of the cord, burying the loop under the stitches. Pull the cord to the wrong side and tie off.

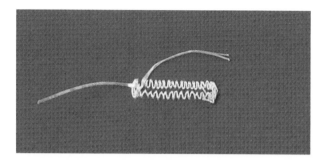

Here is the buttonhole, done with slightly open stitch density at the sides so the cord can be seen, stabilizing the sides.

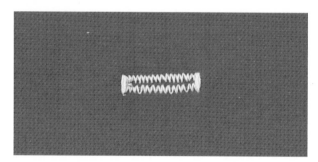

DIY Stretch Buttonhole

If your machine doesn't come with some version of stretch buttonhole (these are usually designed with tiny cross stitches or a stretch zigzag), you can make your own. The process is the exactly the same as the DIY buttonhole (page 126), except that the sides are sewn using one of your stretch zigzag stitches. I like to use the triple stitch, sometimes also called a reverse-action zigzag, for the sides and a standard zigzag for the bar tacks. I think this makes for a pretty sharp buttonhole for mid to heavy knits.

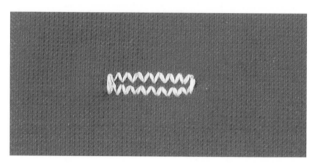

Buttonhole Evasion

There are some times, in some fabrics, for some purposes, or when the sewist has been very traumatized by buttonhole _F.A.I.L._s, that buttonhole evasion is called for. When I am just not feeling buttonhole performance, this is what I do instead.

HIDDEN BUTTONHOLE PLACKET

This is a tricky tactic useful for challenging situations. Rather than making buttonholes right in the garment fabric, these buttonholes are made in a strip of fabric that is then topstitched under the front of the garment. It goes without saying that if you are buttonhole nervous, it is possible to make more than a few of these buttonhole strips before you have one you will use.

1. Cut a long strip twice as wide as the intended placket, plus seam allowances.

2. Fold the placket lengthwise, right sides together, and stitch the two short ends. Turn and press. Finish the long raw edges, generally by turning in and topstitching together.

3. Mark and then make machine buttonholes along the center of the placket.

4. Position this finished placket under the garment front, slightly lower than the neck seam and in from the finished front edge of the garment. Make sure the buttonholes are right on the center front line. Topstitch in place from the right side.

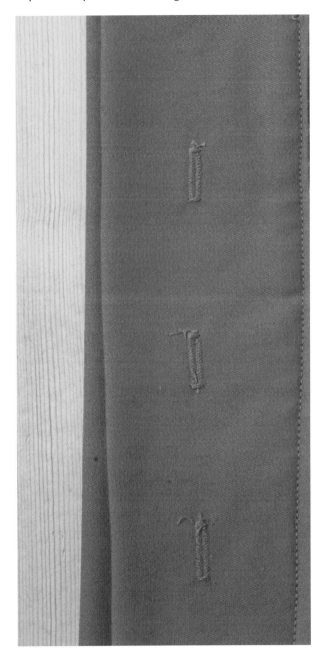

Only the topstitched line will show on the right side of the garment.

5. In a garment that goes right up to just under the neckline, you will need one exterior buttonhole that will show. Fingers simply don't have room up there to get to any button at the top of placket. This one buttonhole is made through all layers. If you think this will be too difficult, consider using a large snap instead, or a hook that can be hidden under a collar.

USE GIANT SNAPS

Sometimes when I am working with a coat or sweater fabric that has a great texture, I just don't want to interfere with it by putting in a buttonhole. I am so glad that large decorative snaps are now available to use as buttonhole and button substitutes.

INSEAM BUTTONHOLES

Sometimes it is helpful to think structurally and not conventionally. Inseam buttonholes are an example of this. In this technique, worked buttonholes are replaced by simple interruptions in a seam. This is an excellent technique for unusual or spectacular fabrics that would just look violated by a machine buttonhole.

Inseam buttonholes do require a button band at the front of the garment. If the pattern doesn't have a band, simply cut back the garment fronts enough to allow one to be sewn in.

1. Cut two garment long band pieces for each buttonhole placket. Cut these as wide as the band plus two seam allowances.

2. Place the band pieces right sides together and stitch down the center (this will be the center front of the garment) leaving spaces in the stitching for every buttonhole.

3. Open this placket unit, wrong sides together. The buttonhole openings will now be in the center of the placket.

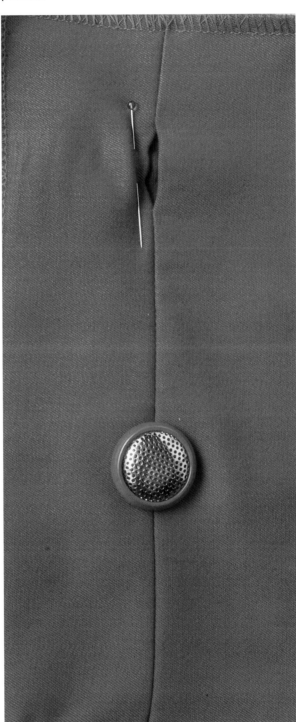

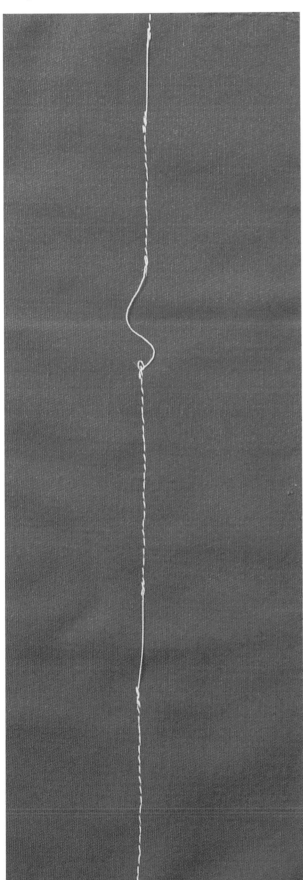

4. Proceed with construction. Sew one side of the band to the garment. Finish the raw edges of the other side of the band by turning the edges under and topstitching.

BUTTONS

Many otherwise relaxed sewists express frustration with their button sewing.

LOOK FAMILIAR?

Despite our best efforts, the back sides of many buttons look messy. It takes a huge amount of care when hand sewing to prevent this.

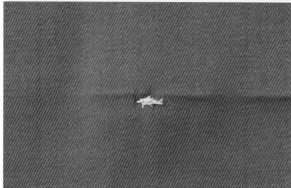

NEXT TIME

I am going to use this space to make a case for sewing on buttons by machine. This is a fast, easy, and most of all neat way to secure buttons.

1. Attach a button sewing foot. Here is one of mine:

If you don't have a buttonhole foot, don't worry. If your presser feet are the snap-on type, just remove the foot and lower the presser bar directly onto the button to hold it still.

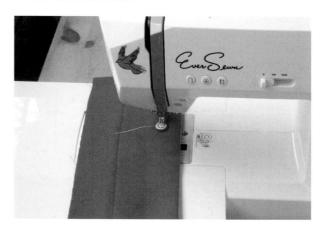

2. Loosen the machine tension so the lock stitch will be hidden on the underside of the button.

3. Adjust the zigzag width to swing exactly in and out of the holes of the button. Set the stitch length at 0, because you don't want that button being moved along by the feed dogs. *Optional:* If you want to sew a thread shank, place a darning needle under the button, between the holes, to elevate the stitching.

4. Lower the presser foot and start stitching. To keep the backstitching neat, start sewing with one stitch, stop, raise the needle and pull the bobbin thread up to the top side. Hold these threads free and to the side while stitching, then pull them to the back side and knot them when you are done. Stitch between one pair of holes and adjust the button to sew the second pair if necessary. Tie threads off on the wrong side.

A button sewn on this way is neat from both the top and bottom.

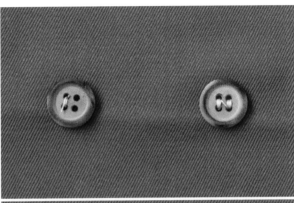

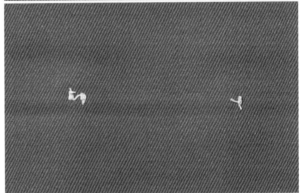

Chapter 9

Hems

A hem is a garment signature, a label worn outside. To me, a hem is the sewist's last flourish. It is a last statement of respect for the nature of particular fabric, and a demonstration of the selection of just the right technique from a repertoire of skills.

It took me a while to get to this place with my own hems. When I was learning to sew, I worried a lot about hems that I was afraid looked "homemade." I did everything I thought I was supposed to. However, too often my hems waved, hung limply, and/or had hand stitches that showed.

Eventually I realized that my mistake was in thinking that there was only one way to "turn up and hem." What a revelation. Once I realized hemming involved a menu of choices, not just one technique, my hemming, and the professionalism of my sewing, took a huge leap forward.

A good hem is the right hem for the fabric and for the style and line of a particular garment. There are many options. Here are the hemming techniques I use most often and the potential problem each one addresses. Enjoy, and relax.

FACED HEMS

The hem of this _F.A.I.L._ A-line doesn't ease in well, and bulk shows from the right side.

WHY THIS HAPPENS

The outer edge of this A-line hem is wider than the skirt. There is just too much fabric to fit gracefully, despite the best easing and pressing efforts.

FIX IT RIGHT NOW

The first step would be to take out the hem and try the conventional advice to run a row of basting stitches across the hem edge and steam this to fit (a process much like easing in a sleeve cap).

Or undo the hem and proceed with the faced hem idea that follows or with a false hem (page 148) if the fabric is thicker.

NEXT TIME

In this process, the hem allowance is cut off and used as a facing. The brilliance of this approach is that this facing will have the same bias in the same areas as the garment and will follow the garment flare perfectly.

Ideally, you have had the opportunity to plan ahead. It is helpful to have enough depth in the hem allowance to add two seam allowances. If not, you will have to sacrifice some of the hem-allowance depth.

1. Determine the location of the hem fold and trim the hem a seam-allowance distance below the fold. If necessary, trim the cut-off hem allowance to the correct height, also including a seam allowance.

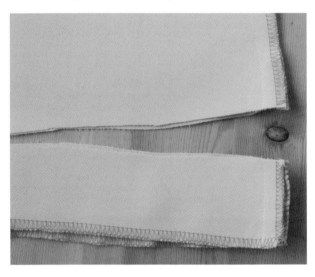

2. Right sides together, pin the cut hem allowance to the skirt. Note any extra fullness in the hem and pin out a new stitching line at any of the seam allowances, taking it in like a dart. Stitch and press.

3. Stitch the hem allowance to the skirt.

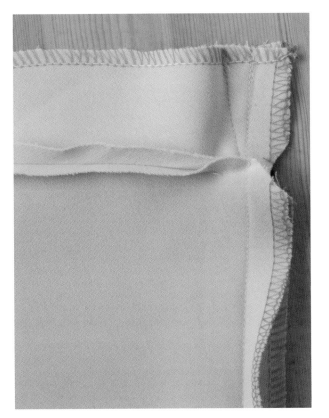

4. Press the seam open and then to the side. Clip the seam allowance so it turns smoothly. Press the facing up, rolling the seam allowance slightly so it is hidden from view on the right side.

5. Hem as usual.

FALSE HEMS

LOOK FAMILIAR?

This bulky hem shows through the garment with a heavy ridge. Trying to press this _F.A.I.L._ made the problem worse.

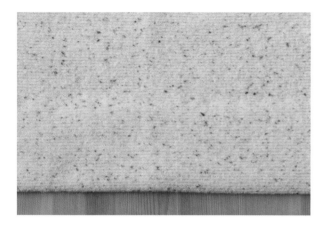

WHY THIS HAPPENS

This is a common issue when hemming thick fabrics and is simply a matter of bulk, not user error.

FIX IT RIGHT NOW

The more you try to flatten this hem, the worse it will get. Best bet is to cut your losses along with the hem. Unpick it, trim the hem allowance down to within a seam allowance distance of the fold, and make a false hem.

NEXT TIME

I love this method and use it all the time with coatings or heavy sweater knits. This is like the faced hem, except this technique involves cutting the new facing from a lighter fabric. I particularly like to use a heavier lining fabric, a slippery knit or woven, to keep the hem from sticking to my legs when I stand up. In the sample below, I used a light cotton interlock to face this sweater knit. Note the difference the false hem makes compared to the conventional hem, seen from both the right and wrong sides of the garment.

SHIRT-TAIL HEMS

LOOK FAMILIAR?

This hem bows out at the side seams. A _F.A.I.L._ on an otherwise great shirt. Note it was also a struggle to control the narrow hem allowance at the side seams.

WHY THIS HAPPENS

The curve at the side seams of a shirt tail hem is largely on the bias, which is prone to stretching.

FIX IT RIGHT NOW

Some fabric needs to be eliminated at this stage. Unpick the hem at the side seam area and unpick the side seam open above it for at least 6˝ (15cm). Press and then trim off some of the curve from the bottom of the side seam. Rehem. Not an ideal solution but probably your best save.

NEXT TIME

Staystitch the hem allowance to freeze the fabric so it won't stretch out at the bias area. However, even this may not eliminate the problem entirely.

For this reason, I do what most manufacturers do. I hem the back and fronts of my shirts before I sew the side seams.

This works so well. The side seam allowances can then be covered with a little tape patch, a common ready-to-wear detail, or topstitched discreetly in place from the right side like I usually do.

UNDERLINED HEMS

A _F.A.I.L._ in fine fabric. Despite my best efforts, the hand stitching in this dupioni hem, as well as the bulk of the serged hem finish, shows through to the right side.

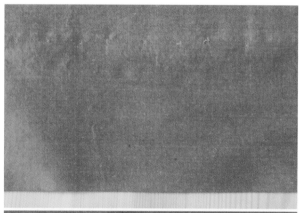

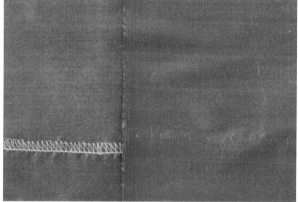

The _F.A.I.L._ conventional hem

WHY THIS HAPPENS

There are many fabrics in which this is an issue. These tend to be the fabrics used in high stakes sewing, such as a dress for a wedding. Fabrics like the ones above are like sewing in glass—everything will show.

FIX IT RIGHT NOW

Unfortunately, there is no immediate fix here. This is one situation that needed to be anticipated. Look at it this way. Any situation that has become a lesson is never a mistake.

Underlining is one of those brilliant techniques that too often is not considered. It's a simple idea—attach a thin fabric to the wrong side of a garment piece and attach any hand stitching to it, not the garment. Underlining is also an excellent way to add a barrier layer between the garment fabric and internal details like seam allowances and darts that might show through to the right side in light fabrics.

1. Cut a duplicate from an underlining fabric—cotton batiste, organza, or just a lining—for each garment piece involved in the hem. Be a little generous with these pieces; anything too small might pull up the garment piece. In the sample, I used china silk to underline the hammered silk dupioni.

2. Baste the underlining fabric to the wrong side of each garment piece. You can do this with a machine basting stitch around all the edges within the seam allowance, but I prefer to use a fast hand baste. Hand basting is looser and more flexible.

3. Construct the rest of the garment, treating the basted underlining and main garment piece as one.

4. Turn up the hem and hand stitch in place, making the stitches in the underlining, not the garment fabric.

The underlined hem, right and wrong side

BOUND HEMS

LOOK FAMILIAR?

The careful hand stitching on this very fine silk still shows. The machine-stitched narrow hem is too stiff for the flow of this fabric in my mind. The effect of both a machine-stitched and a hand-stitched hem would be even more apparent in a translucent fabric like chiffon.

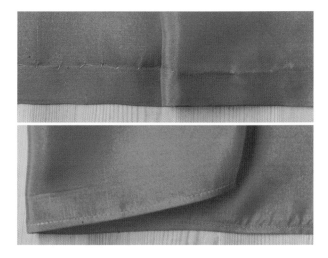

WHY THIS HAPPENS

When the fibers of the fabric are finer than a sewing machine thread, it is really difficult to conceal them or not to let the stitching overwhelm the fabric. It's not you. It's the fabric.

FIX IT RIGHT NOW

Trying again and trying to do it better won't work, plus the fabric is likely to fray as much as your nerves. Best to just cut this off and bind the hem instead.

NEXT TIME

This is a traditional technique that is ideal for fine fabrics. Simply make your own bias binding (see Step 2, page 11) and sew it, right sides together, with a narrow seam allowance to the edge to be bound. Then wrap the binding around the seam allowance to the wrong side and slipstitch (page 168) to secure. The line of machine stitching used to attach the binding will give you a place to secure the hand stitches.

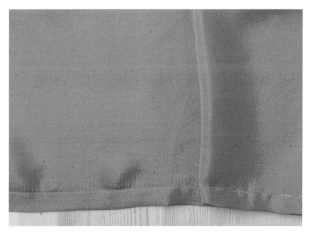

Bound hem from right and wrong side

TWIN-NEEDLE HEMS

LOOK FAMILIAR?

This _F.A.I.L._ twin-needle hem is a classic example of "tunneling."

WHY THIS HAPPENS

Twin-needle hems are made with the bobbin thread, often somewhat frantically, zigzagging back and forth between the two needles. In softer fabric or very stretchy knits, this activity causes the fabric to pull up. That's what makes the tunnels.

FIX IT RIGHT NOW

The only solution is to rip out this hem and start again. Fortunately, twin-needle stitching is really easy to remove. Just run your seam ripper under the bobbin stitches and the hem will pull out very easily.

NEXT TIME

A variety of tactics will fix this problem. A lot will depend on the fabric type, so testing before you commit makes sense. Here is what I would try, in the order I would try it.

Tactic 1: Hand wind the bobbin with wooly nylon thread. Do not wind at the machine—this will pre-stretch it and counteract the ability of the thread to relax under the stitches. The hem below was done with wooly nylon, hand wound in the bobbin. This is how I make most of my own hems.

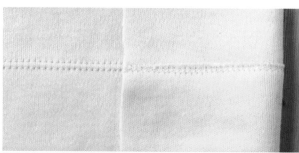

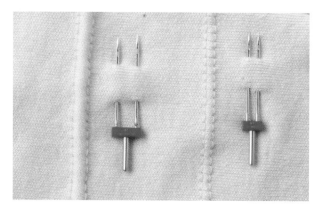

Wooly nylon thread

Tactic 2: Change the width of the twin needle. A smaller space between needles reduces the potential of bobbin pull up. The general rule is the finer the fabric, the narrower the twin-needle space. Note how much flatter the narrower needle hem lies than the wider twin, even though both were sewn with standard thread top and bottom.

Tactic 3: Stabilize the fabric. There are several options.

• *Tear-away or wash-away stabilizer:* The bottom row of stitching was done with stabilizer under the fabric, the top row without, but with wooly nylon in the bobbin. When using a stabilizer, I prefer a wash-away stabilizer. You have to be very careful to avoid the odd pulled stitch, like the one here, when you use tear-away stabilizer.

• *Interfacing:* Find the lightest possible fusible knit, so you have stability without stiffening the hem. Make sure that the stretchy direction is going around the body, like the maximum stretch of the fabric. A very nice hem in my opinion but might not be suitable for very light knits.

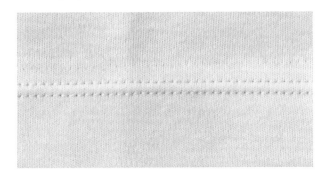

• *Fusible hemming tape:* I have never been a real fan of these tapes because they require heat and I am wary about overpressing, and thus distorting, knits. I also have found that some tapes added a papery stiffness to light knits. However, a friend has been raving about HeatnBond Soft Stretch. So to pacify her, I tried it. Another very nice hem with this, but without the extra volume of the interfacing.

Tactic 4: Sew more slowly. If you have a sew-slow button on your machine, now is the time to use it. Think of that busy bobbin. Give it time to work.

🖊 **For Help with Coverhem Issues**

I considered adding coverhem issues to this list but decided against it. Fine-tuning a coverhem is very machine dependent, and the helpful settings for each model vary. However, many users are very generous in sharing their experience in Facebook user groups. For specific information for your own machine, I suggest you look there.

BLIND HEMS BY MACHINE

Machine blind hems have several characteristics that make them well worth doing for garments that will face a fair amount of wear and tear. Pants, uniforms, children's clothes, or knit garments are good candidates for these hems. Note, however, this stitch and approach to hemming is suitable for fabric with some loft or texture, not for fabrics with a flat finish.

This _F.A.I.L._ is exactly why so many sewists give up on blind hems. The vertical stitches meant to catch the hem are just too obvious, like the absolute worst ready-to-wear.

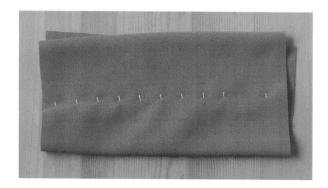

Pretty clear what happened here—the big zigzag in the hemming stitch took a swing too wide and therefore a big bite into the fabric. Tension set at normal, rather than loosened, also meant the stitches pulled up a bit, making them more apparent.

The fix is to take out the machine stitches and try again using the approach outlined here. That's the bad news. The good news is that you can leave the lines of stitching in the hem allowance and just cut through the big zigzags to liberate the hem

Preparing to Sew

There are three components to a nice blind hem:

- **The stitch:** Typically a short run of straight (or small zigzags) interrupted by single large zigzags that swing to the left.

- **The foot:** A blind hem foot has both a ridgelike guide that butts up against the fold (fixed in some versions, adjustable in others) and sometimes also a small finger or wire that lifts the thread slightly so it has some built-in ease when the hem is pulled flat. Loosening the top tension a few numbers helps add necessary slack to the stitch.

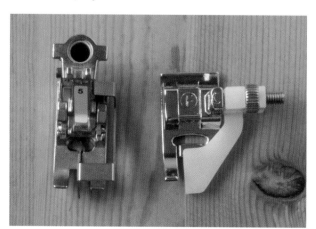

A couple versions of blind hem feet

- **The fold:** The hem is made by turning up a hem allowance and then folding that hem allowance back under the garment to expose just the single layer of hem fabric into which the stitches will be sewn. I generally make and pin the fold in two steps.

1. Fold up the hem and pin along the middle of the hem allowance.

2. Fold the hem under so just an edge of the allowance extends, and pin that in place. For an even hem, it is important to fold so that a consistent width of this single layer is exposed.

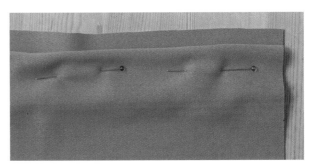

Stitching the Hem

Get the position of the fold guide on the foot and the swing of the zigzag just right. The objective is to let the needle go to the left just far enough for the point of the V of the zigzag to catch only a tiny bit of the hem fold. Experiment with different stitch widths and the position of the fold guide, if yours is adjustable, to fine-tune.

You can see here, on the wrong side of the *F.A.I.L.* hem, how the zigzag cuts quite deeply into the fold.

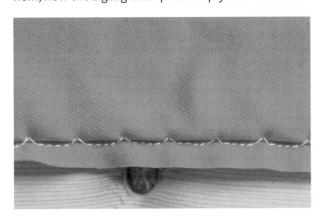

And looks like this from the right side—a durable and entirely acceptable flexible hem for the action-wear knit. In a more textured fabric, the stitch would be even more undetectable.

In contrast, this narrower zigzag catches only a few threads of the fold.

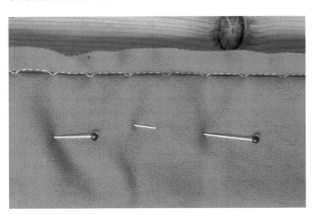

Chapter 10

50 Ways to Relax Your Sewing

If you have gone this far with me, you know my methods are not the generally accepted way to do things. These are my "house" methods for stressless, day-to-day sewing—just my personal tricks for the tricky stuff.

As a result, much of what I have written here is very specific and quite technical. However, an easy attitude when you sit down at a machine is just as important as any how-tos. Here is my list of best practices for laid-back sewing, of course, in no particular order.

1   Don't throw out your scraps until the garment is done. There is some law of the universe that makes facing pieces disappear before they are needed. Anticipate the need to cut out at least one replacement. I have spent enough hours with my head in a stinky garbage bag searching for leftover fabric to make me put this first on my list.

2   Never apologize for your hip number when someone is taking your measurements. Those hips kept you from dying in childbirth. They deserve better from you.

3   Buy yourself ten new bobbins every year on your birthday. No one ever said, "Gee, I have too many empty bobbins lying around here." If you try to wind new thread over old, you are going to run short in the middle of some seam. Then you are going to have to stop and rewind another half-full bobbin that will also run out. Do yourself a favor, have a ton of bobbins on hand. Not to mention it, do yourself a lot of favors. In general.

4   Buy an edge-stitching foot. Yes, of course, you can eyeball an even line of topstitching. But why bother when this foot has such a nice ledge to keep your stitches on track? When you can purchase less stress, do it. See Tip: Accurate Topstitching (page 14).

5   Back to bobbins. Wind more than one before you start. At least two for a half-body garment like a top or a skirt, three for a dress, and four for a coat, five if it is lined. Being prepared will make you feel like a competent person, which is always worthwhile.

6   Consider the undertow effect of social media performance anxiety. You know the *everyone-has-that-pattern-and-is-making-it-so-you-should-too* syndrome. I have a simple self-preservation strategy: If I saw this in a store, would I buy it? This tactic has steered me away from making myself an egg-gathering apron, even though it was so, so cute. I don't have chickens and I can't see anyone around here encouraging me to raise them in the backyard. If that changes, I will be making that apron.

7   Find out if the bride is expecting before you start the wedding dress.

8 Get your scissors sharpened by someone who has a business sharpening knives for chefs or scissors for hairstylists. This is likely a different person than the man who picks them up if they are left at a fabric store. Sharp scissors make cutting out 900% easier and more fun.

9 Own three good seam rippers with good, sharp pointy ends. Realizing you have put the same sleeve in the wrong armhole for the third time is not going to put you in your best mood. Not being able to find the seam ripper when you are already in a snit won't help. Have one you can reach for quickly before you lose your mistake-fixing momentum. Look for the lost one later.

10 Know exactly when to quit while you are ahead. Definitely stop sewing before the "just one more thing" point if you are tired. This is particularly true if the just-one-more-thing is making buttonholes in black fabric past your bedtime.

11 Find the thinnest, sharpest pins you can. Ones labeled "silk pins" are a good start. And look for pins with a colored ball on the end. When they drop on the floor, this will help you find them before they stick in someone's foot.

12 Never sew a shirt for a man who will put it into the dryer. That sort of person will never understand.

13 When someone compliments your garment, don't immediately respond by pointing out your mistakes as in, "I had trouble with the topstitching, see it's crooked here." Instead say things like "I was really pleased with how this turned out." Or even, "Why, thank you." Practice your lines in front of the mirror until you feel smooth enough to accept a compliment gracefully in public. Then go out and do just that.

14 Measure the width of your measuring tape. Many are the width of standard seam allowances. This makes your good old tape very handy whenever you have to add a seam allowance to anything.

15 Get comfortable with some hand sewing. I always run into folks who have taken some kind of pledge to never do anything, ever, by hand. This just seems to be a decision that will add complexity to their lives. A few hand stitches, made slowly when you can see what you are doing (like when making bound buttonholes or installing a zipper in slippery fabric), give so much more control than a sewing machine. Sometimes you need a knife, sometimes a food processor. Same theory.

16 When someone asks you to replace the zipper in a pair of jeans, just look blank, pause, and say no. For this, they invented tailors and neighborhood dry cleaners. However, if they want you to make a whole new pair of jeans—well, that might be interesting.

17 Don't sew over pins. Your first sewing teacher told you not to do this, but, of course, we all do. Hitting pins can bend them into defiant V-shapes, break your needle, and knock out the timing in a machine, which is expensive to fix. The only real way to make sure you don't sew over pins is to place them vertically along the seamline. You'll have no choice but take them out as you go.

18 Know when to walk away. You just can't will the wrong fabric to be right if it isn't. You can't redeem the wrong pattern if it was never meant for a body like yours. Also, there is such a thing as an evil project. Some garments will give you nothing but grief. When dealing with a demonic project, I have found throwing it out of a second-story window is helpful, preferably onto a driveway so you can later back over it with the car. Get that negative energy out of the house, and your head, and move on.

19 Use a pressing cloth. You can use any thin natural-fiber fabric. Just make sure you never use anything packaged and labeled "pressing cloth for sewing." Those are about as useful as a linoleum tile at the ironing board—too thick to let heat and steam pass through. Keep it light, like a cotton batiste or old pillowcase fabric; the job here is to protect the surface of the fabric, not make a barrier to a nice steam press. Pressing cloths absorb all the shine on dark fabrics, the extra glue on fusible interfacings, and scorch marks. That's a lot of stress avoided by not much fabric.

20 Drain your iron after you finish using it. If you have the energy, also let it sit hot for a few minutes to evaporate residual moisture. I have seen enough rusty water eruptions over nice fabric to actually take my own advice on this one.

21 Give up hoping that it will look better when you turn it over. This happens only in pattern guide sheets. If you are going to see it from the outside, sew it from the outside.

22 Mark far more than you feel like doing. If you are someone who often roots around mid-project to find the pattern piece to see where the "large dot" is, it's time to do some prep work. Markings are like street signs along the route of your garment. Actually very helpful.

23 Accept the fact that 95% of all fusible interfacings are horrible (those with glue in big dots or made of nonwoven fabrics), but that 5% are wonderful. Your job is to find the 5% and not be seduced into using anything else. I keep a stockpile of fusible knit for most things, fusible woven cotton for collars, and weft insertion for tailoring.

24 Always use a button with a shank for thick fabrics. A flat button will pucker under the buttonhole. If you have a shankless button you just love, use it, but make a thread shank to compensate.

25 Get an old-school zipper foot, which looks like a skinny little ski, to replace the wide modern one, which looks that a snow shovel. I find the newer, wide versions tend to push the zipper away from the foot and the thin, old-style zipper feet do a much better job of getting the stitches in right close where you need them.

26 Buy a Teflon foot. Teflon feet let even the weirdest fabrics glide smoothly along under the foot, as opposed to sticking and getting caught up under the needle in a big mess. Teflon feet are wonderful for sewing vinyl and leather or anything with a bonded backing, like blackout curtains. Eventually you won't be fast enough and someone in the family will corner you into hemming a pair of those.

27 Remember, you are allowed to make mistakes. If you have learned something, it is not a mistake, it is a lesson. The shirt shown in Chapter 3: Collars and Lapels (page 38) fits the wearer perfectly. I also think I did a pretty good job on the collar, hem, and cuffs. However, after having sewn so many clothes for women, I made this shirt for my son-in-law with the buttonholes on the female side. As an older student once said to me after one of my classes, "Only God is perfect, dear." She was right about that.

28 If someone insists on handing you something to alter, put it on a shelf and forget about it. Eventually that person will move, outgrow the garment, or decide they aren't your friend anymore. In the meantime, you can proceed with lots of interesting sewing in new fabric and new patterns. It's that easy.

29 Own a wire loop turner. The one you want is cheap and looks like a long wire with a tiny latch hook at the end of it. Use it to turn fabric tubes, like spaghetti straps, right side out in about four seconds. The other method involves bleeding fingers, or a thread and safety pin and four days. Your call.

30 Poke around with a couple of cotton swabs in the bobbin area of your machine and up along the needle bar about once a week, if you sew every day like I do. The cotton swabs will pick up all the oily little lint that otherwise will wait until you are finishing a satin prom dress at the last minute and make a black mark at center front.

31 If you ever find you are not enjoying your sewing, ask yourself why, and take action. Are you expecting too much of yourself? Are you just burnt out with production? Even professional athletes have an off season. You are allowed one, too. Nothing wrong with cleansing your palate by hemming pillowcases between mega projects.

32 Use thin, fine hand-sewing needles. Most of the hand-sewing needles in multipurpose packs are just too thick. You will be amazed how much difference a thin needle makes.

33 You don't need to make everything you wear. Sometimes it's good to remember that it is actually still possible to buy clothes. To me, ready-to-wear is like eating out—sometimes I just enjoy the time saved in having someone else do the work. Just because you have the skills to make a bra doesn't mean you have to make one. Do it only if it seems like it would be a lot of fun. If nothing else, ready-to-wear will make you appreciate your own skills, and quality fabric, even more.

34 When you have to thread elastic through a casing, first make a pen mark on one side of the elastic at each cut end. Having these reference marks will help prevent stitching together the ring of elastic with a twist in it—something I did about 874 times before I came up with this fix.

35 Test your old threads, particularly the serger cones. Threads get drier with time. Since dry thread breaks, pull on it before you use it. Better it gives out in your hands than in your seams.

36 Start putting together your own collection of old, faithful patterns, basics that fit you well. It is entirely less stressful, and more satisfying, to add new details to a "tried 'n' true" pattern than it is to start at square one every time. TNTs are also like chicken soup—very soothing when convalescing after sewing a particularly tough or involved garment.

37 Use your serger/overlocker for more than just finishing seams. A serged rolled hem is excellent for thin fabrics. I used it to finish the sleeve vent opening in Chapter 7: Sleeves and Cuffs (page 106). I also love, love the gathering feet for serger/overlockers. These little units finish and gather miles and miles (and just as many kilometers) of ruffles or fabric in minutes, more effectively than many sewing machine attachments. If you are a home-dec person, this will make the tedious job of gathering fun and easy.

38 If the fabric is good, it might be less stressful to recover a disappointing garment than to start new again. I have tried to give you immediate fixes throughout the book. Sometimes just a simple shortening or a bit of waist shaping can rescue a sloppy top. My rule is, if the rescue attempt can be done in under twenty minutes, it's worth a try.

39 Clip to the stitch; don't try to stitch to the clip (page 162). A good place to put this into practice is when you have to pivot at a point, as in Sharp Corners in Yokes (page 54) or The Encased Mitered V, Apply the Band (page 60). The end result is the same, and just so much easier on your nerves than doing it the conventional way.

40 Take just a fraction of a minute when you are starting a seam in fine fabrics, knit or woven, to move the fabric back so the cut edge doesn't disappear down the hole in the throat plate. Fixing those jams is not calming. So, start a little forward, reverse, and then keep going forward. The fancier the machine, the wider the opening in the throat plate and the more important it is to do this.

41 Hold your threads to the back when you start a seam. Obvious, but I often forget to do it. This simple tactic will make for a smooth start, fewer jams, and keeps the beginning of your stitching neat. Might as well start out that way.

42 "Wax" your hand-sewing thread. I annoy myself when I get knots because I forgot to smooth my thread. I don't suggest you actually use beeswax; the residual wax can mark the fabric when pressed. Find a dry bar of soap somewhere in the house and slide the length of thread over it before you thread the needle.

43 Use your hands. I think we sometimes forget that the most powerful tools we have to sew with are our own hands. Try using your hands on either side of the presser foot and sew one hand length at a time when doing the tricky stuff. After you have sewn to the end of your fingers, stop and set up your hands again. This way of arranging your hands is totally different than the one hand at the front to guide and one hand at the back to pull through technique. No need to ever "help" the machine sew.

44 Fit your facings, not your pattern. This is a time- and fabric-saving tip I use a lot. Just cut out the facings and see how they fit around your neck and/or shoulders before you cut out the garment. You will quickly be able to tell if you need to make alterations (like add a few back neck darts) or if this just isn't a good pattern for you.

45 Get some clips. I have recently added sewing clips to the supply drawer next to the machine. I don't use clips for every seam (pins are faster to remove as I sew), but clips are just wonderful to hold knits or slippery fabrics. And because they are stronger than pins, clips are useful when putting a ring of ribbing around a neckline or a circle of elastic around a waistline.

46 Invest in some duckbill scissors. These have one normal looking blade and one blade that, you guessed it, looks like the bill of a duck. The duckbill will keep you from accidentally cutting a little hole in the main garment when trimming. This is good.

47 If you are having trouble with your serger/overlocker, just rethread it. Don't worry about the fact that it seems to be threaded just fine, just do it. Sometimes this will fix a problem you don't understand or can't even see.

48 Laugh. Just don't take yourself too seriously—it cramps your sewing. I remember looking out my window one day and seeing a woman walk by in a "wadder" blouse (page 106) I had donated to a thrift store a few weeks before. She looked great. A real lesson there.

49 Learn to drive-by sew. Keep a machine set up and threaded. Think of sewing as small jobs done on the fly rather than something requiring large chunks of time. I sometimes find thinking of the big picture exhausting. However, I have no trouble with assigning myself mini jobs. (I will just sit down for a moment and pin one seam.) The coat featured in Chapter 5: Pockets (page 68) was constructed in fifteen-minute blocks snatched throughout one week. I hardly noticed the work in this project.

50 Appreciate that there are about 64 ways to do any sewing task and you don't need more than just one that works for you. This book is a collection of my own methods. I certainly don't expect you to love them all. I do hope that what you have read here will empower you to find your own, personalized, customized, best practices. Find what works for your own brain and the feel of your own hands.

Resources

CORE SKILLS

A certain vocabulary of core skills makes sewing so much easier. The techniques listed here will be familiar to anyone who has ever read a sewing guide sheet, but I hope a little more detail on why, when, and how to use them will be helpful.

BASIC TECHNIQUES

Clip

Why

Clips are used to liberate and open up the cut edge of the fabric so a seam can be sewn without pulling, puckering, or catching in tiny pleats.

When

Shapes that curve in, like a neckline, need to be clipped so they can be spread to comfortably fit the straight line of a collar. Pivot points, like the garment side of the point of a V-neckline, or the garment side of a corner into which a yoke or insert is applied, also need to be clipped to avoid caught fabric and puckers.

How

When you clip, cut far enough to make a difference, right to the stitching and staystitching, and often every ¼″–½″ (0.5–1cm) along a curved edge. The test for a curved neckline is that it must be clipped often enough so the neckline can be pulled straight.

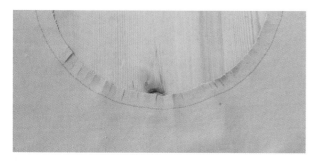

When clipping to a pivot point, it is far more effective to clip to the stitch than it is to stitch to the clip, as is standardly advised. Try this instead.

1. Stitch to the pivot point, often identified in the pattern as "the large dot."

2. At the pivot point, put the needle down. Raise the presser foot.

3. Using small scissors, clip close to the last stitch at the needle. Here the fabric has been removed from the machine so you can see clearly where the needle would stop, needle down, directly at the pivot point.

4. Pivot the fabric, lower the presser foot, and finish the seam.

Tip How to Prevent Fraying

If you are worried about fraying at the point of the clip, iron a small piece of fusible interfacing to the area before you sew. I generally use a lightweight knit fusible for this. I find that interfacing is more effective than staystitching, which patterns often suggest.

Grade

Why

Seams along pressed edges need to be graded, one seam allowance trimmed shorter than the other, to reduce the potential for seam-bulk show-through on the right side of the garment. Think of grading as making steps along a seam so the allowances will blend into the garment more smoothly.

When

The edges of collars, cuffs, and facings need to be graded before they are pressed.

How

The trick with grading is knowing which seam allowance to make shorter. Fortunately, it's an easy rule to remember—the wider seam allowance, the shield, is the one away from the body; the shorter seam allowance is the one next to the body.

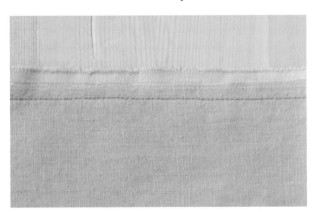

In situations where this can change mid-seam, along a lapel line for example, the choice of longer seam allowances will switch at the break point where the lapel turns back. The wider seam allowance will be next to the jacket body before the break point, next to the lapel above it.

Notch

Why

Notches are cut out of the seam allowances along curves that curve outward. Removing these tiny triangles of fabric eliminates bulk that would pack up and make little lumps along the seamlines when turned to the right side. Be aware that many pattern instructions say to clip these curves when really, they need to be notched instead.

When

Outward, or convex, shapes that require notching along the seam allowances include rounded shaped collars, like the Peter Pan or shawl, and patch pockets with curved corners.

How

Use small, sharp scissors and notch more frequently along the areas of greatest curve.

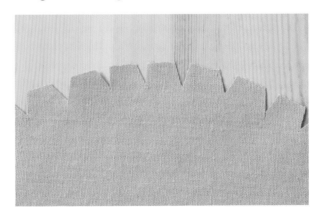

Understitch

Why

Understitching is an excellent technique for preventing an edge of fabric from rolling through to the outside where it will show.

When

Typically, facings are understitched along necklines, armholes, and fronts below the roll line. Some sewists also understitch the long edges of under-collars to keep them tucked under. This is a good technique to use at your own discretion whenever you feel a stitched edge needs to be securely kept out of sight. I have sometimes staystitched along the inside of faced hems (page 146) or false hems (page 148) if I felt a slippery fabric made this necessary.

How

1. Sew the facing or other unit to the garment and clip and grade (page 163) the seams as required.

2. Press the seam open and then to the facing side.

3. Working from the right side and using your fingers to keep the seam allowances next to the facing and not the garment, stitch the facing to the seam allowances, close to the seamline. In many cases, it might not be possible to stitch along the entire seam. Getting into some corners can be tricky; don't worry about that, just do your best.

USEFUL HAND STITCHES

Backstitch

Why

The backstitch is a structural stitch used to sew strong seams by hand. This makes it a particularly handy stitch for situations that are difficult to reach by machine, when repairing a canoe for instance, or finishing those last few stitches at the end of a hard-to-reach seam. I completely love backstitches!

When

Backstitches are extremely useful when attaching patch pockets from the wrong side of a garment, for many mending jobs, or for executing or completing small, tricky seams. When done by the practiced hand, the right side of a backstitch can be almost indistinguishable from a row of machine stitches. It can be harder to make the backside as neat, and you might want to consider this when deciding to place backstitches where they will show.

How

Backstitching is very easy to do and exactly as advertised.

1. Start with the knot on the wrong side of the work and bring the needle up through the layers of fabric.

2. Instead of moving forward with the next stitch, push the needle back down through the fabric, but behind where the needle first came up.

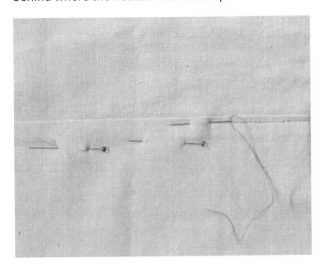

3. Bring the needle up again through the fabric, a stitch length ahead of this first stitch. Push the needle back down to meet that stitch and continue. Here is what the stitch looks from the right and wrong sides.

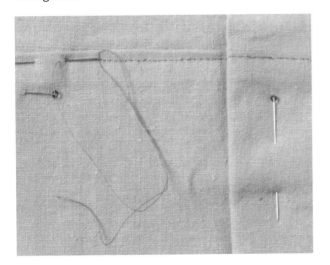

Catch Stitch

Why

The catch stitch is a wonderful stitch. It is essentially a herringbone stitch worked toward the right if you are right-handed, and to the left if you are left-handed. This stitch is flexible and less likely to break than a slip stitch (page 168).

When

The catch stitch is a great all-purpose utility stitch useful for hems (because it has flexibility, it's suitable for both knits and wovens), and any situation where securing an edge without pulling or puckering matters. Catch stitches can be used to tack down facings at seams and to apply nonfusible heavy interfacings or interlinings, among many other uses.

How

Working toward the direction of your dominant hand but the with the needle pointing away from the direction of the stitching, make little X's between the edge and the garment. Be careful not to pull the thread too tight to avoid pulling up the fabric.

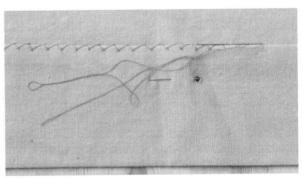

Fell or Felling Stitch

Why

The fell stitch is one that dressmakers have adopted from tailors, and not surprisingly use it most in their own tailoring work. Felling refers to a stitching process where small, vertical stab stitches are made around the perimeter of a piece to securely attach it to the garment, much like appliqué. Felling stitches are tiny and have some mobility. This makes them an excellent choice for neatly attaching fabrics without pulling or puckers.

When

Use a felling stitch to apply a felt under-collar (see Option 2: The Brilliant Menswear "Felt Under-Collar" Method, Step 9, page 50), for appliqué work, attaching linings to the inside of garments, or to apply lace or other trims to edges. It is also used extensively in tailoring to apply stay tapes along roll lines and stress seams.

How

Felling stitches are made very much like slip stitches with these exceptions:

• The edge of the material to be applied, folded or cut, is attached with tiny vertical stitches, visible on the edge.

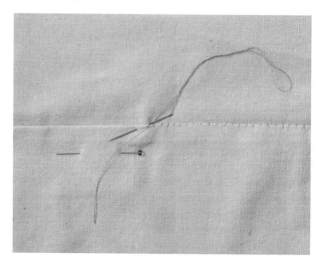

• Instead of hiding the needle under the hem or edge as in slipstitching, the needle is inserted, and hidden, in the garment fabric between stitches. This is the secret of the fell stitch's strength. Here is what the stitch looks like from the right and wrong side.

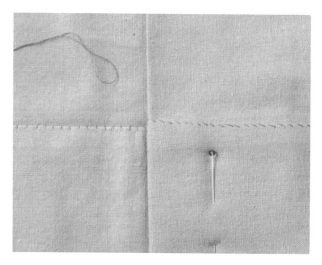

Prick Stitch

Why

The prick stitch is a beautiful version of the backstitch, almost as strong but far more elegant and
even easier to do. Unlike the more utilitarian
backstitch, the prick stitch is used primarily as a
functional topstitch.

When

Most modern sewists use the prick stitch to sew in a
zipper by hand (see Alternative to a Machine-Stitched
Zipper, page 105) or for topstitching on patch pockets
or other details in delicate or lofty fabrics that might
look violated by machine stitching.

How

The process is sewn from the top of the garment.
It is identical to that used to make a backstitch
(page 164), except that in Step 3, the needle is
pushed back down into the fabric only a small
distance behind where the stitch came up rather
than to meet the preceding stitch.

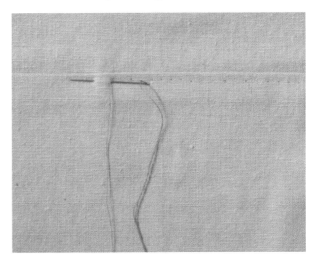

This is what the stitch looks like from the right and
wrong sides.

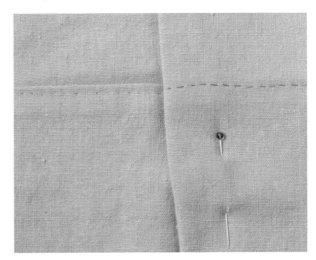

Slip Basting

Why

There is more than one way to baste. Slip basting is my favorite kind of construction basting. It is capable of holding things still, often so much more effectively than the conventional in-and-out stitch.

When

Slip basting is most useful when working to set things up on the right side of a garment. I use it to hold down patch pockets, to close up welts or the lips of a bound buttonhole, and to make perfect lapped zippers (see Lapped Back Zipper, page 96).

How

A nice slip baste isn't rocket science. Simply make big, loose diagonal hand stitches between the two units you want to hold together.

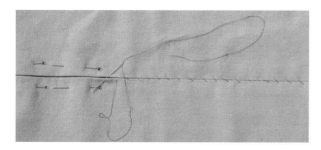

Slip Stitch

Why

Unlike the catch stitch, in which the thread is very visible, a slip stitch is used when detail or edge attachments need to be as close to invisible as possible.

When

Hems can be slipstitched, but this stitch is more appropriate for invisible jobs, such as attaching linings. It can also be used to apply the edges of patch pockets to the front of a coat or jacket that will be secured later from the wrong side with a hand backstitch. Whenever an old-school pattern instruction says, "Sew invisibly," they are telling you to slipstitch.

How

There is one trick to near invisible slipstitching—hide the needle and you will hide the thread. Slip stitches are worked away from your dominant hand with the point of the needle in the direction of stitching.

1. Take the first stitch in the edge to be attached, in this example a hem. Make sure the knot is hidden behind the hem allowance.

2. About ½″ (1cm) or more away, take a tiny stitch in the garment, ideally catching only a thread or two.

3. Then, and this is the important part, hide the needle under the hem allowance and let only the tip pop up. Take a tiny stitch in the hem and then directly above it another thread or two in the garment.

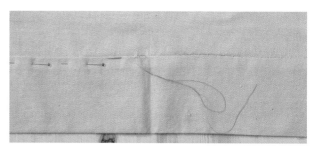

Staystitch

Why

Staystitching freezes a cut edge so it doesn't stretch out of shape (which can substantially distort the line and even size of a garment) with handling or during construction.

When

It is important to always staystitch along any woven curved or sloped edges like necklines and shoulders in which bias may make them vulnerable to stretching. It is also a good idea to staystitch along cut edges of woven fabrics that by themselves stretch out easily, like bouclés or other loose weaves. To be effective, staystitching should be made directionally with the grain moving from the widest to the narrower edge. For example, stitch a front scoop neckline in two stages down from each shoulder to the center front.

How

Observing the direction of stitching, place the staystitches just inside the garment seamline. Use a shorter stitch length and do not backstitch at either end of the stitches to reduce thread bulk. Below, the turquoise stitches are staystitches.

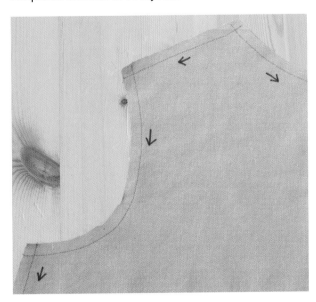

Swing Tack

Why

The swing tack attaches garment units and details securely but with built-in mobility. Swing tacks tend to be useful anywhere that layers need to move a bit with the wearer, but with stitches that won't pucker or tear.

When

I use swing tacks all the time. I use them to attach hanging linings to coats or skirts at the seams, near the hem allowances. They can also be used to connect the sleeve linings to the garment at three places (front notch, shoulder seam, back notch) inside the garment.

How

Depending on the scale of the garment, the swing tack acts as a sort of bridge between two garment units. For a coat or jacket for example, a swing tack is usually about 1″ (2.5cm) or less in length. There are several options for making them.

• Use a doubled thread and go back and forth between the two units, 3 or 4 times. Secure each end of the tack securely with a few stitches. This is the classic swing tack.

• Do the above but cover the length of the tack with hand worked buttonhole stitches. This is often called a thread bar.

• Alternately, you can save a length of serger-tail run off after a rolled hem, thread it into a large-eyed needle, and make the tack out of that. Or you could crochet a chain out of heavy thread and secure the ends with a few stitches.

GARMENT NOTES

Chapter 1 (page 8): Lakeside pajamas by Grainline Studio. Blue-and-white striped cotton seersucker. All edges of this set are finished with self-fabric bias binding. To make construction even simpler than the pattern, the shorts can be made by sewing the center front and center back seams and then binding all edges. The side seams can then be overlapped and topstitched down.

Chapter 2 (page 22): Cadence dress by Love Notions Sewing Patterns. Curry yellow linen with cotton print facing. I made the tank bodice with the all-in-one facing and omitted a waist casing.

Chapter 3 (page 38): All Day Shirt by Liesl + Co. Gray lightweight cotton chambray. Classic men's shirt details, with the stand collar technique described in this chapter. This man's shirt has all the correct details of a classic shirt: stand collar, flat-felled seams, and shirt-tail hem, but nearly all the traditional techniques have been changed up for something easier, faster, and stress free.

Chapter 4 (page 52): Vintage Stretch and Sew knit rugby top #301, lengthened to a dress. Purple dotted cotton/LYCRA* with patterned contrast placket.

LYCRA is by INVISTA.

Chapter 5 (page 68): Vogue 1479. Hunter green boiled-wool coat. Flannel-backed Kasha lining. Back also underlined with chamois leather for additional warmth and to cut the wind. Zippered pocket in lining on left side. Exterior double-protected patch pockets and vertical hand-warmer welt pockets.

Chapter 6 (page 90): Style Arc Mindi skirt in denim. Center front zipper, zippered slot pockets. The pattern's original pockets were patch pockets with a zipper applied to the top edges. I decided to change these to inset zipper pockets for a smoother look.

Chapter 7 (page 106)**:** Style Arc Catalina dress and top. Coral polyester, self-covered buttons. I added a silk/cotton lining for comfort. Invisible zipper in the back. Bound hem. If I made this in the shorter, blouse version I would probably eliminate the zipper and leave the top of the center back seam unstitched to make an opening that would be closed with a button to match the sleeves.

Chapter 8 (page 124)**:** Butterick 6107, stand-up collar coat, view C. Heavy, embossed red boiled wool. Since this coat was unlined, I added a satin false hem, and I hand-stitched a chain to add weight along the hem edge to prevent the coat from sticking when I stand up. Bound buttonholes and protected patch pockets.

Chapter 9 (page 144)**:** Tessuti Fabrics Sadie slip dress, shocking pink silk, bias cut. Narrow bound hem.

Index

About the Author

Barbara Emodi sews every day in Halifax, Nova Scotia, Canada. She has taught her techniques for stress-free and satisfying sewing online and in person in Australia, Canada, and the United States.

She is the author of *SEW … The Garment-Making Book of Knowledge* and has written extensively for many sewing magazines. She is also a past contributing editor of *Threads* and for many years wrote a regular column for *Australian Stitches*. Barbara has gained even more followers as a course instructor on the innovative and interactive platform Creative Spark Online Learning (by C&T Publishing).

In addition to her sewing, Barbara is a regular political commentator for CBC Radio (Nova Scotia). In her past life as a political communicator, she often traveled with a small sewing machine in her briefcase for emergency stress relief.

Photo by Karen Veinot

Visit Barbara online!

Blog: barbaraemodi.com

Creative Spark:
creativespark.ctpub.com

Also by Barbara Emodi:

Creative Spark

The perfect marriage of in-person teaching and online learning:

Self-Directed
Work at your own pace from the comfort of your home

Lesson Level
Instructor Discussions
Ask questions as you go

LIVE Events
Ongoing LIVE Events with our world-class Instructors

What are you waiting for? Join us and Elevate Your Love of Crafts!

CREATIVE SPARK
ONLINE LEARNING